Investing in the Stock Market

THE NO NONSENSE LIBRARY

NO NONSENSE FINANCIAL GUIDE®

Investing in the STOCK MARKET

Gerald Warfield

Longmeadow Press

Dedicated to my uncle,
Orville H. Slaton
of Mineral Wells, Texas

Cover design by Nancy Sabato

Interior design by Richard Oriolo

ISBN: 0-681-41393-X

Printed in the United States

First Edition

0 9 8 7 6 5 4

CONTENTS

ONE

Buying and Selling Stocks

What Exactly Are You Buying?

Stocks are units of ownership in a cooperation. By law, a corporation must divide itself into such units (or **shares** as they are also called). No matter how many or how few are created, the total number of shares issued represents the total ownership of a corporation, and you may own all or part of any corporation simply by owning its shares. Some corporations may issue only a few shares, but most issue many thousands, even millions.

All the shares of a corporation are created the same size. If you own a hundred shares of IBM, that represents the same amount of ownership as a hundred shares owned by any other person. Some corporations have issued more than one type of stock so that the different issues might be evaluated differently—and we'll see a couple of those cases later—but in general, one share in a company represents the same amount of equity ownership in that company as any other share. This also means that as the value of a company increases, the value of all its shares increases proportionately. The converse, of course, is also true.

Advantages and Rights of Stock Ownership

Investing in stock has several advantages. One is that most stock can be sold quickly and efficiently, and for a profit if the market price has gone up. Another is that along the way some of the company's profits can filter down to you in the form of stock dividends.

It is also your right as a stockholder to receive a stock certificate if you want one. Most people have their broker keep their securities, but you are entitled to your very own certificate with your name on it if you want it. (Recently some brokerages have started charging a $15 fee for preparing these certificates.)

A much touted benefit of stock ownership is voting. Every year investors are mailed a ballot and proxy form along with the announcement of the shareholders' annual meeting. Shareholders are asked to vote on new board members and on important issues to come before the meeting or to give their proxy to someone appointed by the board who will vote for them. The average investor owns such a small percentage of any one company's stock as to make the return of the ballot or the proxy form seem only of academic interest. However, there have been cases where stockholders banded together and successfully wrested control of a company from a recalcitrant board. This is done by someone soliciting (and obtaining) the proxies of a large number of shareholders and then voting with those proxies against the board at the shareholders' meeting. **A proxy fight**, as such a struggle is called, is not the norm and usually requires the leadership of one or more major stockholders like the manager of a mutual fund or a giant pension fund. But more important than how often it is used is the fact that it is there; it constitutes the power of the owners over management, and it *can* be used. Sometimes the mere threat of a proxy fight is enough to effect change in a corporation.

Here is a complete list of your legal rights as a shareholder:

As a Shareholder You are
Legally Entitled to:

1. a stock certificate
2. the right to sell your shares, or buy more
3. a dividend if one is declared
4. information, everything from an annual report to looking in the corporate minutes
5. maintain your proportional share of ownership, that is, if more shares are issued you have first dibs on some of them
6. vote for the board of directors and on any fundamental changes in the corporation
7. share in the assets in case of dissolution

The Importance of the Number of Shares Issued

Let's take the case of a corporation that issues a thousand shares (and we'll assume those are the only shares the corporation has ever issued). If you buy 100 shares then you will own a hundred thousandths (100/1,000 or ten percent) of the company. That's a big stake. You would be a major shareholder and might even get a seat on the board of directors. If another company of the *same size* issued a million shares (instead of only a thousand as our first company did) and you bought 100 shares of that company, then you would have bought only a hundred millionths (100/1,000,000 or a hundredth of one percent) of that company. Each share of the second company would theoretically be worth only a thousandth of the value of the shares of the first company. The point is, the more shares a company issues, the less each share is worth because the corporation is being divided into smaller and smaller pieces.

It's called **dilution**, and in principal it's very simple, but of course, things aren't so neat and tidy in the real world. Determining the value of a stock is at the core of investing and subject to a myriad of technical and emotional factors. Nevertheless, all the data you see about a stock, its price, its earnings per share, even its dividend will be affected by or calculated from the number of shares the company has issued.

The Marketplace for Securities

Creating stocks and transferring the ownership of those stocks from individual to individual is complex and requires careful regulation by the participants in the market, by regulatory agencies, and by the government of the country within which these transactions take place. Some countries do not permit ownership through publicly owned shares, and in those countries either no stock market exists or it is very rudimentary. However, the system has proven so useful and so practical that even in the remaining communist countries limited stock markets have appeared. In China, for example, small securities markets have cropped up in several of the major cities although mostly government bonds are sold there.

Public ownership of stock dates back to Amsterdam in 1602 and the owners the Dutch East India Company. Civic minded as these gentlemen might have been, they didn't create stock just so people less wealthy than they could get a piece of the action; they did it for a purely practical reason: to raise money. Ships were expensive, and outfitting one for a journey halfway around the world was a major risk. They needed investors to share in the expense and in the risk. Furthermore, they figured that if they could sell off part of their company and get funds to expand operations then the pieces of the company they retained for themselves would eventually be worth even more.

In addition to offering their shares for sale it was necessary to arrange for those shares to be easily bought and sold by future investors. This is a concept called **liquidity**. In the case of the Dutch East India Company you bought in by paying the previous owner and signing the company register. You could sell just as easily. A marketplace for bonds and for currency exchange already existed in Amsterdam at the time, and so the new securities began to trade there. (That's the basis of Amsterdam's claim to having the first stock exchange.)

Four hundred years and a lot of technology later we're still trading securities basically the same way—and for the same reasons.

Where Does the Stock on the Exchange Come From?

Stock bought on a stock market comes from the previous person or institution that owned the stock. The shares are not owned by the stock exchange, but more important they aren't owned by the issuing corporation, and the corporation doesn't get any money from the transaction. Then how does a corporation raise money from the sale of stock? From the **initial public offering.** When stock is first issued, the purchases of the shares are from the company itself (through a stock-broker intermediary). Those shares are not sold through a stock exchange. After all of the new issue has been sold the company gets no more money no matter how many times the stock is later sold and resold.

That's an important point. Stock exchanges are places where the stocks that are bought and sold are not owned by the issuing company. By far the majority of securities transactions are of this type, and they make up the **secondary market**.

The Securities Market Is Divided Into:

The **primary market** where the stock is sold for the first time (and the issuing company gets some money). The **secondary market** which is every other sale of that stock for as long as it exists, which is probably as long as the company exists.

So that's what a stock exchange is for, the secondary market.

How Do You Buy Stock?

You buy stock through a stock broker. Using a middle man irks some investors, but brokers are a godsend to others. Later on, a whole chapter is devoted to brokers, but for now, here's what you do. You first decide whether you want investment advice or not. If you are going to make all your own investment decisions, whether from your own research or from an investment letter, then you'll want a discount broker. You call them, give them your order, send them a check, and that's that. Discount brokers simply act as clerks and are cheaper than full-service brokers.

If you want advice or help in selecting an appropriate investment you should use a full service broker. They are more expensive (typically 2% to 2 ½% of the dollar amount of the transaction) but they attempt to steer you to the right investment given your financial circumstances and your investment goals. They also can help you decide when to buy or sell.

In either case you must establish an account with a broker. The account itself doesn't usually cost anything. The broker only charges you when he or she performs a transaction for you. You will receive monthly (sometimes quarterly) statements from that broker listing your holdings, their value, and any transactions such as sales, purchases, receipt of dividends, etc. It is usual for the broker to hold all your securities for you. There are several advantages to this practice, called holding your securities in **street name**, the most important being convenience. You won't have to mail the stock certificate back to the broker by certified mail every time you make a sale. Your broker can also hold any securities that are registered in your name; that service is called "held under safekeeping."

Your broker will funnel through to you the annual and quarterly reports from corporations in which you hold shares. You may also get other services from a broker like up-to-the-minute price quotations on the telephone. Even discount brokers offer this service.

You can open basically two types of accounts with a broker: a **cash account** is the simplest. You pay for what you buy. Usually you have five business days to pay for your purchases. A **margin account** is one in which you may make purchases on credit using as collateral the stock you presently hold in that account or the stock you are buying. Such purchases are considered loans and you pay interest on the outstanding balance until it is paid off. You should be aware that owing money on your stocks adds to them another element of risk. If you are just starting out, best stick with a simple cash account. In a cash account when you sell, the broker sends you the proceeds or holds it in an interest-bearing account until you decide to reinvest.

When Do You Sell?

When to sell is fully as important as when to buy, and you should retain control here just as when you made your original purchase. If you allow circumstances to dictate when to sell—for instance, when you need money—then you are almost guaranteed to lose money in the stock market. The point is that the funds with which you invest in the stock market should be funds you don't have immediate need for. The stock market is no place for money you know you'll need in three months. Park those funds in a CD or money-market fund, not in the stock market.

Why Invest in Stock?

The corporation dominates free-market economy because it provides a mechanism whereby businesses can raise the capital to grow, and at the same time puts the benefits of that growth within the grasp of the average citizen. Extension into major markets far exceeds the resources, physical and monetarily, of the individual. Yet by means of dividing ownership into small segments and selling those segments to the public, the resources of individuals can be pooled creating an atmosphere favorable to the growth of corporations.

Buying corporate stock is a prudent way to increase your wealth, and about 25% of adult Americans are attempting to do so in just this manner. If you have some discretionary funds—and you should if you are thinking about investing in the stock market—you have any number of choices you can do with your money, but studies repeatedly show that in the long run stocks can be counted on to outpace inflation and other investments. That means that with reasonable diversity and judgment you can increase the buying power of your money over the long run.

Is there risk? Yes. But there are common-sense guidelines to help you. The three keys to successful investing are reasonable diversity, investing for the long term, and being informed enough to take advantage of opportunities before they become obvious to everyone else.

Before you total your profits, you have to see if you made enough money to pay your commissions, pay your taxes, and keep up with inflation on the principal amount. But that's not as hard as it might sound. Millions do it—whether they're trying merely to keep their nest egg from shrinking because of inflation or to make a killing in the market.

Want More Information?

Write to the New York Stock Exchange for their free *Investor's Information Kit*, New York Stock Exchange, Inc., Publications Department, 11 Wall Street, New York, N.Y. 10005. They also publish a yearly fact book (price $10.00).

There's also the **American Association of Individual Investors** whose aim is to educate investors. They publish a magazine and various specialty reports and booklets. Write to them at 612 North Michigan Avenue, Chicago, IL 60611.

Kinds of Stock

Common Stock

There are two broad categories of stock: **common stock** and **preferred stock**. Common stock is by far the more prevalent and will be considered here in detail. Preferred stock is a rather special security and will be described briefly later in the chapter. When the terms "stock" or "shares" are used it is always assumed that the reference is to common stock.

Only corporations issue stock. An individually owned proprietorship like a beauty parlor or a delicatessen cannot issue stock. Neither can partnerships like your local law firm or an architecture group.

Incorporation is always within a specific state, and the

number of shares is specified in the Certificate of Incorporation. The board of directors of the corporation can, and
usually does, increase the amount of stock at a later date,
and, despite the risk of dilution, there are many good reasons
for doing so: the most important being that selling stock is an
efficient way to raise new capital when it is needed.

Stocks are usually bought and sold in lots of 100. This
is called a **round lot**. That's not to say you can't buy three
shares or eighty-six shares, but sometimes the price will be
higher, usually by ⅛ (twelve an a half cents per share), called
an **odd-lot differential**. The purchase of shares in other than
100-share lots or multiples thereof is said to be an **odd lot**.
Brokers usually have a minimum transaction fee so that if
you are considering buying only a few shares of a company
you should check that the minimum brokerage fee will not be
so high proportionally as to make the purchase unprofitable.
Surprisingly, full-service brokers sometimes charge less than
a discount broker for small purchases.

Dividends

Dividends are the disbursement of profits to the owners of the
company, that is, to its shareholders. It's one of the advantages to being an owner rather than someone who has simply
loaned the company money (a bondholder).

It is up to the board of directors to decide on the
dividend. If a company has a million shares outstanding and
makes a million dollars profit in one year then there is one
dollar in profit for every share outstanding. In this case the
board of directors might decide to reinvest or retain half the
profits and to pay out the other half to the shareholders. That
means there is now a fifty-cent dividend for each share.

Shares usually pay dividends quarterly, that is, every three months, so the shareholders would receive a fourth of fifty cents (7.25 cents per share) every three months. For five hundred shares that's $36.25 every three months ($.0725 x 500).

When your securities are held by your broker, the dividend will be credited directly to your account there. Usually brokers invest such funds immediately in a money market fund so that your money earns interest while it is waiting for reinvestment or disbursement to you. There is no brokerage fee for handling your dividends. That is one of the services you can expect from a brokerage house whether it is a full-service or discount house. If you have the stocks issued in your name and you hold the certificates or if they are held under safekeeping at your brokers, then the dividend check will be mailed directly to you at the address the company has on file for you.

Sometimes a company will go into debt to meet its dividend payments. This is particularly true for older, larger corporations that have a long dividend history. However, that can be a danger signal. Unless a corporation has a good reason (like the promise of increased profits or productivity right around the corner), then the price of the shares may soon be dropping. You may lose far more in capital when you sell the shares than what you gained in interim dividend payments.

But just because a dividend is lowered or even skipped doesn't mean that you are hanging onto a loser. The priorities of the company may change; a major acquisition may have taken place; all kinds of reasons can hurt the dividend. If this happens to a stock you hold, find out why. Call your broker. All he or she has to do is punch that security up on their terminals and there will be a news item about the change of the dividend. If you read a financial daily or weekly you may read an article about it long before the dividend is due. There will also be an explanation in the quarterly or annual report you receive from the corporation although that will be long after the fact. Evaluate for yourself whether you think the change in dividend is reasonable, whether it indicates poor health of the company and whether you should continue to hold the securities.

The dividend is a major reason many people chose some stocks over others. Besides the chance for the shares to appreciate you receive dividends along the way, and that's particularly important when you hold shares for a long time. For instance, if you held shares for four years and sold after they increased in market value 20% that's only 5% profit per year. But if you received an annual 5% dividend in the meantime that increased your total return to 10% per annum.

The Dual Attraction of Common Stock:

The combination of **cash flow** through dividends and **capital gains** through price appreciation.

Dividend payments are seldom as high as interest payments such as from bonds. That's because bonds are loans. The bond holder receives only the interest on the money loaned and the return of the principal when the bond matures. In fairness to bonds it is true that capital gains are possible if the bonds were bought at a discount or if falling interest rates increases the market price of the bond (see chapter 11) or if the bond's credit quality improves. But in general, bonds are not the instrument for capital gains.

Comparing Bonds to Common Stocks

Bonds offer more cash flow per annum since interest payments are usually higher than dividends. However, there is less chance for capital gains and no chance of an increase in cash flow in the future.

Not all stocks pay dividends. The board of directors may be investing all the profits back into the company for future growth which should eventually be reflected in a higher market value for your shares. If you are investing solely for capital gains, that is, to sell later at a profit, then you may want to invest primarily in such stocks, called **growth stocks**. If you want a combination of income and capital gains then high quality common stocks are for you.

Limited Liability

A major benefit of stock ownership which is usually taken for granted is limited liability. Basically that means the investor who owns stock in a company cannot be held responsible for the debts of that company. The total risk to the investor extends only to the amount invested, no more.

As the sole proprietor of a grocery store, an individual can be liable for the debts of that store. In fact, if the store gets in real trouble the owner might have to liquidate some of his other assets and even be forced into personal bankruptcy. The same risk can be incurred in a partnership.

The concept of limited liability developed gradually in

free-market countries. Approved by the British parliament in
1855, it was slower to take hold in the U.S. As late as the
1930s stock in some corporations, banks for example, still
carried with them kinds of liability such that if the bank failed
stockholders had to pay any outstanding obligations.

Limited liability is absolutely fundamental to the way
the stock market functions. Without it the risk of owning
stock would simply be too great for small investors, and the
market would only be a place for institutional investors and
the wealthy.

Preferred Stock

Preferred Stock has been described by some as a cross
between stock and bonds. Typically it has a higher dividend
rate than common stock, and that rate is fixed at the time of
issue. Unlike common stock where the dividend is subject to
yearly ratification by the board of directors and changes
according to the fortune and priorities of the corporation,
preferred stock has a fixed dividend or an "adjustable"
dividend which changes according to fixed parameters.

On the company's balance sheet preferred stock appears
as debt, which means, among other things, that preferred
shares do not constitute equity ownership like common
shares. From this perspective they look more like bonds. On
the other hand, preferred shares do not mature like bonds,
and there is no mechanism for the refund of the par value.

Preferred shares are typically issued by utility companies and banks as an alternative to other types of debt
financing. While you may not own any preferred shares
yourself, it may be important for you to know of their
presence. For example, if you hold common shares of a

corporation that has also issued preferred shares then you should know that the dividend of preferred shares has precedence over your dividend from the common shares. The obligation to pay the dividend to preferred shareholders comes right after the obligation to pay interest on bonds. Only after both of these obligations are met do the board of directors dole out the remaining money to the common stock holders.

If a corporation is unable to pay the dividends of preferred stocks, sometimes those dividends are cumulative. That is, the obligation to pay remains, and if the company becomes more solvent at a later date the full back dividends must be made up before any dividends on common shares can be paid.

The disadvantage of preferred shares is that their market price does not move like common shares. This is because the dividend will never be increased as it can be for common shares (assuming that the company did well). So with preferred stock the dividend is safer than with common stock, but the chance for capital gains is less—like a bond.

Warrants

Warrants are a type of stock substitute that also trade on the stock exchange. They allow the holder to purchase a limited amount of stock in a corporation at a fixed price for a stated amount of time. Since the market price of stock constantly fluctuates, an instrument such as a warrant can become valuable if the current price of the underlying stock rises above the fixed price guaranteed by the warrant.

The market value of a warrant is decided in part by the price at which you are allowed to buy the underlying stock.

When a warrant permits you to purchase shares below market value then the warrant takes on intrinsic value in addition to their purely speculative potential. For instance, if you had a warrant that allowed you to buy 100 shares of a stock at $5 a share that was currently trading at $7.50 per share then the warrant would have intrinsic worth of $2.50 per share since you could turn around and sell the underlying stock for $2.50 more than you paid for it. The current market price for that particular warrant would be even more than $2.50 difference since the underlying stock still has the potential of rising even farther.

Warrant certificates often come with a new issue and are good for five to ten years. They are intended to increase the attractiveness of a new issue by offering the possibility of additional capital gains at a later date. When warrants come with a new issue the stock/warrant combination is referred to as **units**. For example, a unit of XYZ Corporation costing $10 might include one share and one warrant. Lets say the warrant enables the holder to buy 100 shares of XYZ for $15. The warrants aren't worth much except as speculation until the market value of XYZ's stock rises above $15. Four years later, when the common stock of XYZ is trading at $20 the warrants are worth at least $5 per share. If investors liked the stock and wanted to add it to their portfolio then conversion into common stock would be appropriate at this time. However, if the warrant holders only wanted to take a profit, then they would not usually convert the warrants to stock just in order to sell them on the market. The easier way would be to sell the warrants since the price of the warrants would have been tracking the higher price of the stock they could be converted into.

Warrants can be detached from the newly issued stock certificates and traded separately. Currently there are 17 issues of warrants trading on the New York Stock Exchange.

Want More Information?

The Consumer Information Center distributes a booklet published by the U.S. Securities and Exchange Commission entitled *What Every Investor Should Know*. It covers common stock, preferred stock, warrants and other financial instruments. Write to them at P.O. Box 100, Pueblo, CO 81002. They also distribute a free booklet of their own entitled *Before You Say Yes: Fifteen Questions to Ask About Investments*.

THREE

Anatomy of a Stock Market

S tock exchanges exist to facilitate the trading of stocks and other securities such as bonds, warrants, and options. A stock exchange does not sell securities itself, but simply provides a place where such securities can be bought and sold. This entails bringing the buyers and sellers together and providing enough support equipment (like computers and advanced communications networks) to facilitate the trades.

Stock exchanges generate income from fees charged to the brokers who utilize their facilities and by small commissions charged on each transaction (again, paid by the brokerage firms). Even so, the New York Stock Exchange is a not-for-profit corporation, and the revenues it earns are only to pay costs. All stock exchanges are regulated by their own regulatory boards and by the Securities and Exchange Commission, a government agency that administers the Federal securities laws.

The largest and most prestigious exchange in the U.S. is the New York Stock Exchange. The volume traded on this exchange is enormous, estimated at more than 75% of the dollar value of all common stock publicly traded.

Only securities specifically listed on an exchange are allowed to be traded on that exchange. Generally, corporations aspire to have their securities traded on the New York Stock Exchange, partly because of the prestige, but also because of the visibility and instant access to the deepest pockets in the investment world. Each exchange has requirements for listing and not surprising, the New York Stock Exchange's rules are the most rigorous. These rules cannot guarantee that any company so listed is a good investment or even currently in good financial condition, but at the time of admission it must have met certain requirements of capitalization, longevity, number of shares in public hands, and so on.

Requirements for Listing on the New York Stock exchange (Abbreviated):

1. Earnings of $2.5 million
2. Net tangible assets of $18 million
3. Market value of shares at least $9 million
4. Publicly held shares numbering at least 1,100,000
5. At least 2,000 stockholders.

Stock markets are not markets in the ordinary sense like a farmers' market where you would go to buy apples. It's more like a place for getting all the people together who want to buy apples and all the people who have apples to sell and putting them together in a corner and letting them thrash it out. It's called a two-way auction market. Buyers compete with buyers to get the lowest prices and sellers compete with sellers to get the highest prices. Needless to say, such a system works only when there are a lot of buyers and a lot of sellers.

Just how does the stock market get all the buyers and sellers in the same corner? It's done through the specialist system. Brokers who have a seat on the exchange (that is, who have purchased the right to do business on the exchange and have been approved to do so) are assigned to oversee and regulate the buying and selling of the stocks of several companies. That broker is the specialist for that stock, and all other brokers wishing to buy or sell on behalf of their clients must come to that specialist.

Such a system has been criticized as being an inefficient bottleneck, but over the years the specialists have done remarkably well, on the whole. Their most important job is to keep the price of a security as stable as possible. When there are lots of people wanting to buy and not so many wanting to sell the price goes up. When it happens the other way around the price goes down. Also, the specialist maintains a large inventory of the stock in his own account to use when necessary to balance the supply and demand. It would seem cumbersome, perhaps, because if you have demand for a million shares and only 500,000 are currently offered for sale where do you get the rest? What happens is that the specialist raises the price and a few more brokers show up wishing to sell. If there is not enough, maybe the specialist throws in some of his own stock, but if he sees it is clearly not enough, he raises the price again until more brokers show up to sell. Often the stock that becomes available to sell is the result of **limit orders**. The specialist might have on his books an indication that if the price of XYZ stock gets up to $35.75 a share then broker A wants to sell 100,000 shares. If it gets up to $36.00 then broker B has 500,000 shares he wants to unload, and so on. Currently, about 20% of the total share volume involves specialists buying or selling from their own accounts.

Large trades on the stock market are called **block trades** and executed for large institutional investors like mutual funds and pension funds. Such trades are of interest to the average investor only insofar as they have the size to begin to move the price of a security. A single block trade will usually be at the current price level but several combined with an increase in smaller trades will begin to move the price. Sometimes these trades are made off the floor and handled by firms that specialize in trading large blocks of shares.

The second-largest of the U.S. Stock exchanges is the American Stock Exchange, also located in New York. It is based on the specialist system, like the New York exchange, but the traders use open outcry in their trades so that the specialists participate far less in the trading, often only recording the transactions.

The other exchanges are all regional such as the Pacific Stock Exchange with a trading floor in San Francisco, the Midwest Stock Exchange in Chicago, the Philadelphia Stock Exchange, the Cincinnati Stock Exchange, and the Boston Stock Exchange.

Sometimes your broker may tell you that he or she executed a trade on a regional exchange because of a marginally better price. This is common practice among brokers, and there are a whole breed of traders who look for small price discrepancies between exchanges and instantly leap in with a purchase and a sale. They hope to simultaneously purchase securities on one market at a fractionally lower price and sell on another at a fractionally higher price. The timing and funds necessary make this an activity for professionals only. These traders are called **arbitragers**. They serve a useful function, equalizing prices between markets more efficiently than any regulatory agency could manage it.

As you can imagine, volume of the magnitude on the NYSE must be organized and executed by means of computers. The specialists have whole banks of computers that execute small orders automatically, keep them informed of the balance of supply and demand, advise them of price fluctuations on other markets and of orders and limit orders waiting to be executed. What specialists end up doing is fine-tuning this flow. They are governed by exchange regulations stipulating the increments by which they can raise or lower prices and the circumstances by which they can do so. If the supply and demand get hopelessly out of balance then trading in a specific security may be halted for a period, even for the rest of the day, the hope being that the buying or selling frenzy will settle down and an equilibrium in the market be reached. Sometimes the exchange disseminates news or information that explains the sudden demand before allowing the stock to reopen.

Currently on the New York Stock Exchange:

1. a total of 2,284 issues are listed, 110 of which are foreign
2. the total number of shares is 90.7 billion
3. the total value of shares is $2.8 trillion

What Happens to Your Order?

There are elaborate stories about how orders are transacted on the New York Stock Exchange. But unless you are a very large investor, your order for 500 shares of XYZ will only be a blip on a computer at the specialist's station. Volume on the exchange is so great that your order will simply join all the others efficiently processed electronically. That's not to say that if demand exceeds supply that the price won't go up, but your order won't do it. You'll have to be a part of a veritable tide of orders to begin to move the price.

It is possible that your broker will have an inventory of some stocks and won't have to go to the exchange for the security you wish to purchase, but that is the exception rather than the rule. It is also possible that your broker will purchase the security over-the-counter (which we'll go into in the next chapter).

When you place an order with your broker, the brokerage wires the order through to its own station and onto the specialist's computer (this assumes the brokerage has a seat on the exchange). The specialists stand at places called booths. If it is a very big order (over 12,000 shares) a broker, called a floor broker, will take the order over in person and negotiate the transaction face to face. Traditionally, he doesn't say whether he's buying or selling but simply inquires about the price of the security. The specialist will give two prices: a **bid price** that is the current purchase price for the stock and the **asking price** which is the selling price. There might be a quarter of a point difference between the two prices. This difference is called the **spread**. When there is lots of activity the spread will be small, when there is not much demand the spread will tend to widen.

There are some corporations that don't like having their securities handled through the specialist system. There is no doubt that the specialists have a lot of power, and they have no competition, so alternate markets, alternate ways of transacting the purchase and sale of securities, have developed. The most important of these is the over-the-counter market.

Want More Information?

The two major newspapers that cover every aspect of the stock market are *Barron's* which comes out on Monday ($2.50 an issue) and *The Wall Street Journal* which comes out every business day ($.75 a copy).

FOUR

The Over-The-Counter Market

O ver-the-counter refers to the fact that at one time securities not listed on an exchange—and this included respectable stocks like banks and insurance companies—were purchased at a broker's office literally over the counter. Today, it still refers to securities not listed on an exchange, but the trading is far from over-the-counter. Perhaps over-the-computer would be closer to the truth.

The over-the-counter (OTC) market is enormous. Thousands of corporations have their stock sold in this fashion, and the mechanism grown up to accommodate these trades is very sophisticated, in many ways more modern, more competitive and more forward-looking than the organized exchanges. In fact, features of the OTC system were recently incorporated into the new design of the London Stock Exchange.

This is how an over-the-counter transaction takes place. You inquire about price through your broker. He or she punches up that security on their quote terminal. The quote terminal checks the ticker, which gives the last price at which the security traded; it also flashes the current best bid and best ask prices. (There are, in fact, other bid and ask prices, but the system is geared to show only the lowest ask price and the highest bid price which is what your broker would want to see.)

The posted prices are from **market makers** anywhere in the country, that is, brokerage firms buying and selling that security for their own account. If you agree to the ask price or bid price given, depending on whether you are buying or selling, your broker sends the transaction through to the firm's order department.

In newspaper quotations you get the impression that there is only one price for stock. In fact, even on the exchanges there are two, the bid price and the asked price, but the paper may only quote the price at which an actual sale took place, called a **transaction** price.

A large number of market makers post their prices on the quote system. In fact, behind every bid and ask price there are typically a host of other market makers ready to buy at a fraction of a point lower or to sell at a fraction of a point higher. If your broker ever tells you there are only three or four market makers for a stock you want to buy, you should reconsider that purchase. When there are only a few market makers competition diminishes and the spread between the bid and asked price can become unusually wide. For some issues the spreads can reach 50% and even 100%, and under those conditions it becomes increasingly difficult to sell at a profit since the bid price has to rise farther to overtake the ask price.

For lower-priced issues a healthy spread between a bid and ask price can be as low as a sixteenth of a point. For higher-priced issues the spread can be a point or more, but when the spread gets beyond a point check with your broker to make sure that there is, in fact, a liquid market for that issue. Sometimes spreads of several points will appear for units, but in those cases the price is usually above $20 and the units include more than one share or have warrants attached.

There are several advantages to the over-the-counter market system. The most important is that the competition between the brokers makes for the best prices possible. And if the trading is lively, there will be a very small spread between the bid and ask price—always the sign of a healthy market for a stock.

OTC Price Quotations

Transaction prices are quoted for some OTC stocks, exactly like exchange issues, but some quotations list bid and ask prices. The bid price is the price a market maker is willing to pay, and the ask price is the price a market maker is willing to sell. Sometimes only a bid price is given.

The regulating agency for the over-the-counter market is the National Association of Securities Dealers, and quotations are reported by means of the National Association of Securities Dealers Automated Quotations Service, called NAS-

DAQ. You will see quotations in the newspaper for NASDAQ securities; all are over-the-counter. They have a **national list** which includes the most actively traded stocks. In major papers their national list quotations are as comprehensive as those of the New York and American Stock Exchange.

Minimum requirements for listing on the NASDAQ system are at least two market makers, $2 million in assets, and a capital surplus of $1 million. Companies of this relatively small size, however, will be listed only on what are called the pink sheets and their quotations will not be generally available except by asking a broker. Stocks appearing on the national listing will be of much larger corporations. When you purchase over-the-counter stock be sure to find out in what NASDAQ listing the quotation is to be found.

Penny Stock

No discussion of the over-the-counter market would be complete without consideration of so-called "penny stock." The term is variously applied to stock selling anywhere from five dollars to pennies a share.

There is money to be made in this market—primarily by brokers selling penny stock during a bull market. The securities are highly speculative, volatile, and in need of constant watching. No brokers are as aggressive as the salesmen for penny stock, especially for new issues of untried companies. The abuses of telephone salesmen hawking new issues of penny stock became so great that the SEC has recently initiated a "cold-call" restriction on these brokers. The rule requires that the brokers obtain basic financial data from potential customers and fill out a form showing that the penny stock is an appropriate investment. This rule can be circumvented if the penny stock is listed on an exchange, and so there has been a recent trend by corporations issuing penny stocks to try to get their securities listed on a regional exchange. The Philadelphia Stock Exchange has been a favorite of these small companies in that it has suspended its listing requirements several times to admit penny stock issues.

After the initial offering of penny stock is sold and the issue begins trading on the secondary market its price can drop like a stone. If you are brave enough to speculate in this area, it is crucial to have a broker with whom you do a lot of business and who will advise you carefully. Make it clear that you will be a continuing customer so that more is at stake than a quick sale. Be prepared for most of your trades to lose money. The best strategy is to bail out as soon as the price starts dropping, and purchase a variety of stocks so that your winnings will offset your more numerous losses.

Some people, of course, dream of the penny stock that will bloom into a major listing on the New York Stock Exchange. But for every one of those securities there are fifty that lose money for their buyers.

Information about the
Over-the-Counter Market

The National Association of Securities Dealers puts out a *NASDAQ Fact Book* with statistical information on all aspects of the over-the-counter market. The booklet is free. Write to NASDAQ, Inc., 1735 K Street, NW, Washington, DC 20006. You may also obtain a *NASDAQ Company Directory* which lists all NASDAQ companies, their addresses and their ticker symbols for $5.

Blue Chip, Cyclical, Growth, and Other Stocks

The categories of stocks we will consider in this chapter are not actual types of stock like common and preferred. Instead they are categories into which investors and analysts have grouped securities in order to characterize their behavior in the marketplace and their suitability for different investors.

Blue Chip

These are the shares of large, well-known companies that have a record of sound earnings, regular dividends, and strong price performance. Blue chip stocks are for long-term investing, and they are usually high-priced. Their value will decrease the least in a down market, and the companies that issue these shares will think carefully before trimming their dividends. In short, blue chip stocks are the nearest thing to a sure thing on the stock market.

The down side is that large corporations—which blue chip companies inevitably are—may have reached their limits and be more concerned with maintaining current market share than with growth. This is understandable since it would be much harder for such a company to double in size than for a medium-sized company or a small company just starting out.

Blue chips are solid but not very exciting. If you are just starting out in investing you may want to purchase companies with more growth potential. Nevertheless, even in the most aggressive portfolios a core of blue-chip stocks, say 10 to 20 percent, is a good idea to provide some hedge against a downturn in the market. Think of them as a safety net in case your riskier investments don't pay off.

That having been said, you can lose money in blue chip stocks just like every other kind of security. In a recession all stocks fall, but blue chips might not fall quite so far. In a bull market blue chips always do well, but not as well as growth stocks.

If you are investing for income, preferred stocks, bonds, and blue chips with high dividends are for you. Particularly with respect to dividends there are three important things to consider. The first is the financial strength of the company. Ask your broker how *Standard & Poor's* rates the corporation financially. Next look at the **payout ratio**. Those companies that pay out the least of their earnings in dividends are in the best shape to raise their dividends in the future. And finally, check the **price-earnings ratio**. This is the ratio of the market price of the security to the per-share earnings of the company. The P-E ratio, as it is called, will be considered in detail in chapter 6, but in general, remember that the lower the P-E ratio the better. For example, you are safer buying a stock that sells for only eight times its earnings than a stock selling for twenty times its per-share earnings. You can find the P-E ratio in most newspaper stock quotations.

No criterion for stock selection can be mindlessly applied without interpretation. For instance, the news that a company is expecting substantially lower earnings might have caused the market price of its securities to fall. The lower price of the common stock would have caused the P-E ratio to fall, too, because the P-E ratio is calculated on past earnings. In this case the lower P-E ratio would have to be discounted in any assessment of the stock.

A comparison of payout ratios and P-E ratios will be most meaningful between the stocks of companies in the same industry. This is because expectations for both these ratios are different depending on whether the corporation is in insurance or cosmetics or whatever. More will be said about the comparison of stocks later in this chapter.

Investing For Dividends?

The payout ratio is a good measure of the safety of a stock's dividends. It's the dividend divided by the net per-share earnings minus preferred share dividends. Usually shown as a percentage, the lower that percentage the more likely the company can increase the dividend in the future.

Growth Stock

These are stocks with more promise than substance. They may be perfectly sound companies but the expectation of investors is that the market price of their securities is going to appreciate faster than the shares of more mature companies. As always, when there is more potential reward there is also more risk. If the expectations of investors are not eventually met, then the price of these securities can fall quickly. The company may be perfectly sound, it is only investors' expectations that need be thwarted for the bottom to fall out.

An important point about growth stock is that the projected increase in market price is based on an expectation of increased earnings. Seldom does growth stock have the fundamentals immediately in place to justify its price, so that the shares always look expensive. This is typical of companies with a new product or a new drug or those in a fashionable industry like waste management. The expectation is that the company's earnings will grow more quickly than other companies and thus the high price will eventually be justified.

Growth stocks seldom pay dividends, or if they do they pay only two or three percent of their earnings. The companies are putting all their resources, probably including hefty debt, into the development of new products or new markets or research or whatever. It is typical for a prudent investor to have some of his or her portfolio in growth stock so that they can participate in favorable market conditions, but no more than ten or twenty percent. If you are investing for income, then you don't want growth stock at all. If you are young and have cash you don't need right away, then a portfolio of predominantly growth stock might be for you. However, be sure to have plenty of diversity because in a portfolio of primarily growth stocks you will have some losers. What you want is to cut your losses soon if a stock heads south and to let your winners ride. You are counting on your winners more than balancing out your losers.

Undervalued Stock

Undervalued stock is often confused with growth stock and yet they are nothing alike. The investor attitude toward undervalued stock is that it has no potential at all. Usually it is a company that has been in existence for a long while and is doing reasonably well, or just plodding along, and no one expects it to break out from the pack.

Typically an analyst might, in going through the financial report of a corporation, find that accounting procedures caused some asset to be depreciated more than they should have been or to be undervalued in some other way. Often investment newsletters will speak of hidden assets.

If the price of the security hasn't already risen by the time you get word of an undervalued stock, then this would be an investment to consider. Buying undervalued stock is far less risky than buying growth stock. All growth stock has going for it is expectation, and its current price is way ahead of its performance. Undervalued stock, on the other hand, usually has tangible assets or potential in place but yet to be recognized. That's not to say that the share price of undervalued stock can't drop, too, but it is less likely because there has been no investor expectation to be thwarted. Some investment newsletters specialize specifically in finding undervalued securities.

One virtue you will need when acquiring growth stock is patience. Obviously you will have to wait until other investors also recognize the value of your stock for its market price to increase.

Cyclical Stock

The prices of cyclical stocks get periodic boosts from the economy, business cycles, or the whims of fashion. You are best to be cautious of cyclical stocks unless you know an industry well or have advice from a reliable source. Traditionally cyclical stocks, like autos and chemicals, usually bottom out in recessions, so if you buy them when the economy is bad, by the time the economy improves, so has your investment.

The timing of cyclical stocks is everything. Just because their market price is currently low does not mean that they will not go lower or that the economy will be such that your stocks will do anything but sit in the doldrums for years.

Special Situations

When something happens to a company independent of the business cycle, the economy, and so on, that might cause the price of its shares to rise dramatically then you have a special situation. The most common special situation is a takeover attempt where a company starts increasing its holdings in another company—buying huge quantities of stock—in order to effect a takeover. The price increases are often quick and precipitous. The best situation to be in is to already own this security. You might get an offer to purchase your shares from the rival company or you might simply be able to sell your shares in the market for a substantial profit.

Getting in on the action when you don't already own the stock is a bit more tricky. There are plenty of traders with one eye on their quote terminal, one eye on the news, and both ears to the grapevine. The average investor can't hope to beat such traders to the draw. A quick in-and-out might net you some profit, but it's risky and you have two quick commissions to deduct from your profits. Usually after you hear of a special situation the price has already adjusted to investor expectation.

There are some analytical techniques especially geared for spotting takeover targets, and there are some investment newsletters that specialize in anticipating takeovers. If you do invest in this area then you will want to spread the risk around. Have a diverse collection of shares because they will not all be winners. Undervalued companies that are pinpointed as potential takeover targets are probably your best bet so that if the anticipated takeover does not materialize you still have a security that might be "discovered."

Evaluating Stock Within an Industry

If you are contemplating the purchase of a particular stock it is always an excellent idea to look at other stocks in that industry. The reasons for this is that it will give you some basis for the evaluation of the stock you are considering. What if it has an usually high P-E ratio? If all the stocks in that industry traditionally have a high P-E ratio, like stocks in the pharmaceutical industry, then you discount that as a negative factor in your evaluation of the security. Likewise, if it has usually low debt-to-equity ratio, you might discount that as a positive factor if all the companies in that sector have generally low debt to equity ratios. When your broker recommends a stock to you, ask how it compares to other stocks in that industry.

Investment Advisory Services

These two investment letters have become industry standards. Both are comprehensive and both are expensive. Your local library is likely to subscribe and your broker's office will have copies for you to consult. Both are weeklies.

Value Line Investment Survey evaluates over 1,700 stocks with respect to financial stability, expected performance, risk, dividends, and many other criteria. Geared toward the experienced investor, the price is $395 per year. Write 711 Third Avenue, New York, NY 10017 or call 800-633-2252.

Standard & Poor's Outlook evaluates stocks on the basis of risk and investment goals. It lists and rates best and worst performing stocks and stock groups. Projects economic trends and industry forecasts. The price is $195 per year. Write 45 Broadway, New York, NY 10004.

SIX

Keeping Informed (Quotations)

Newspapers all the way back to colonial times have published the prices of securities. Today, even in a high-tech world of television, quote machines, and cellular telephones, newspapers remain one of the major sources of information on stocks, bonds, and other securities. If you are investing for the long term, newspaper quotations are certainly adequate for your purposes.

Most newspapers have pages devoted to financial quotations, so the first thing to do is find the right tables. You will see quotations for stocks, bonds, options, commodities, futures and government securities. Sometimes there are as many as seven different listings for stocks: NYSE, AMEX, three NASDAQ lists, one list for regional exchanges, and one for major foreign exchanges. Both the New York, and the American Stock Exchange tables may be titled "composite listings." This only means that the prices quoted (and volume) include all trading on other exchanges where the stock might also be traded.

The three over-the-counter listings can be particularly confusing. One is called the National Market or the NASDAQ National Market (remember that NASDAQ stands for the National Association of Securities Dealers Automated Quotations, which is the quotation service for over-the-counter issues). Almost 5,000 stocks are in that listing, which is made up of the largest and most frequently traded issues. Often papers only print abbreviated versions of that list. Also, papers will omit any stock that didn't trade during the period covered by the quotations. The second list, sometimes called the National List is shorter and made up of smaller companies. The third list may simply be called "Bid and Asked" prices or "over-the-counter." When you purchase an over-the-counter security be sure to ask your broker under what heading the stock is quoted in the newspaper.

Newspaper Stock Listings

New York Stock Exchange (NYSE)

American Stock Exchange (AMEX)

NASDAQ National Market

NASDAQ National List

NASDAQ Supplemental List (or just Bid and Ask)

Regional U.S. exchanges (or other U.S. exchanges; sometimes Canadian exchanges are listed here, sometimes separately)

Foreign exchanges (or overseas markets)

Most newspapers in the U.S. get their quotations from the Associated Press, and there is an understandable uniformity. The format varies from paper to paper only in what information is included. Here's a sample of a complete quotation:

52-Week High	52-Week Low	Stock	Div	Yld %	PE Ratio	Sales 100s	High	Low	Last	Chg.
26	20	PeopEn	1.72	7.0	12	236	25¼	24½	24⅝	− ⅜
17¼	8⅜	PepBoy	.13	.9	22x	1545	14	13⅝	13¾	− ⅛
35⅝	21	PepsiC s	.48	1.6	21	16735	30	29½	29⅞	+ ⅛
31⅜	18⅝	PerkEl	.68	2.4	19	489	28⅜	27⅞	28⅛	...
18¾	11¼	PerkF	1.30	7.2	14	100	18½	18	18⅛	− ⅛

If the first two columns of a stock table are numbers, as they are in this example, then they are invariably the 52-week highs and lows: the highest and lowest prices paid for that stock in the previous year.

The 52-week high for Pepsico (abbreviated PepsiC) is 38⅝. That means the highest transaction price for the parent company of Pepsi Cola® in the last year was thirty-eight dollars and sixty two and a half cents. Numbers with fractions like this confuse people into thinking that they may not be dollar prices since ⅝ doesn't divide evenly into $1.00. But all numbers in stock quotations that refer to prices are points interpreted to mean dollars. The quotations for low-priced issues even utilize sixteenths and thirty-seconds. Here's a little table to make the conversion of some of the eighths a little easier:

Dollar Conversion for Fractions	
⅛ = $.125	⅝ = $.625
¼ = $.25	¾ = $.75
⅜ = $.375	⅞ = $.875

The value of the 52-week highs and lows is that you will know whether the current price for which the security is selling is near the top or bottom of the price range for the year. That alone is not enough information on which to make an investment decision. You have no way of knowing whether a security selling at a 52-week low is selling at a bargain or if the price deserves to be that low and is still heading lower. However, when buying undervalued stock (see chapter 5) just knowing the range of price over the last year can give you an idea of whether the security has still been overlooked by most analysts. An "undervalued" stock selling at a 52-week high has probably been discovered by someone.

Incidently, the 52-week high and low is always adjusted if something happens to make those prices misleading. Consider the case of a stock split when the number of shares is increased. If it were a 2-for-1 split then for every share you used to own you now own two. The value of the shares is therefore halved. To accommodate the split the prices in the 52-week high and low are also halved. In the example, you see an 's' after Pepsico indicating that such an adjustment has been made.

The Abbreviation of the Corporation Name

Right after the 52-week high and low comes the name of the corporation issuing the security. Obviously, the newspapers would not have space to print the full name of all the companies, so abbreviations are used. There is nothing sacred about these abbreviations. They are dreamed up by the Associated Press, and they will be changed if the company requests it, say, if the company thinks another abbreviation would be clearer.

It doesn't take much plowing through the quotations to realize that the abbreviations of a great number of securities simply are too short for the name to be easily figured out, and given the space limitation there probably isn't even a reasonable alternative. Some are easy enough, like GenElec for General Electric, but what about CrmpK? It's a hopeless mess, trying to figure out all those names, but you have to take into consideration the way quotations are usually read.

Most people don't run down a stock list like they were looking for bargains in a supermarket ad. Investors turn to the quote tables for the current prices of securities they are already interested in. If you own shares of Crompton Knowles and want to know what it closed at yesterday, then you already know what you are looking for. When you get to the "Cr's," the abbreviation CrmpK suddenly takes on a bit more meaning. The same for Advanced Micro Devices. When you get to the "Ad's," the abbreviation AdvMicro is quite clear.

Sometimes additional abbreviations follow the name. Here are some of the more common ones:

pf = preferred stock

pfB = preferred stock issue "B" (or A or C, etc.)

wt = warrants

n = a new stock issued within the last 52 weeks. The 52-week high and low indicate prices only as of the start of trading.

s = The stock has split. The 52-week high and low have been adjusted to reflect the stock split depending on the ratio of the split.

The Ticker Symbol

Here's where names can get a little confusing. The ticker symbol is *not* the abbreviation used in the newspapers. Ticker symbols must be shorter, no more than three letters for New York and American Stock Exchange issues, no more than five for over-the-counter stock. No way can three letters, even five, intuitively denote the myriad of companies in the stock tables.

But intuitive or not, the ticker symbol is a constant. It is assigned by the exchange or by NASDAQ and it is an iron-clad way to specify a security. Always, always, always get the ticker symbol of the security you purchase from your broker. When you receive your confirmation, the ticker symbol should be there, too. Use it when placing orders and there will never be any confusion about what security you are talking about. Unfortunately, most newspapers don't have the room to include the ticker symbols in their daily quotations.

Sometimes they do in weekly tables, but the best source for ticker symbols is the *Wall Street Journal*. It gives them right after the abbreviated company names under the column heading "Sym."

Sometimes ticker symbols have extensions, a period followed by additional letters. That's sometimes part of the symbol, too. A period followed by "Pr" indicates preferred stock. If there is more than one class of common, then period "A" would indicate common class A or B or whatever. Sometimes the additions indicate entirely different instruments such as warrants ("WS"). One common extension of ticker symbols is "XD" meaning ex-dividend. GM.XD would mean that General Motors was trading ex-dividend on that day. (See Dividends below.)

It may seem strange to you that many people can sit in a brokerage office and watch the ticker tape or—more common today—watch the ticker on the financial news channel. How can they remember what all those symbols mean? But people watching the ticker never know all the symbols. Like the abbreviations example earlier, investors know only the symbols for the handful of stocks they are following.

Incidentally, it is expected that a person following a security on the ticker knows the general price range within which that security is trading. This enables the ticker to take some short cuts in order to save space. For instance, if XYZ security has been trading somewhere around $25 a share, the ticker would only show XYZ5¼ meaning the transaction was $25.25, or XYZ4⅞ meaning that the trade was as $24.875 per share.

Dividends

The next column usually shows the dividend. Most large companies in the U.S. pay dividends quarterly. (There are some exceptions where dividends are paid less frequently such as foreign stock which tend to pay bi-annually.) The figure you see listed is the anticipated annual dividend given the quarterly dividend. Thus if you see the dividend listed as 2.4, meaning $2.40 per year the quarterly dividend would be $.60 per share per quarter. A person owning a round lot would receive a check for $60.00 every three months ($240.00 ÷ 4)

Most qualifiers tend to appear on either side of the dividend amount or the sales figure. You should check the newspaper key for their meaning but here are a few examples:

Dividend Qualifiers

a = the amount in the dividend column includes extra payments made in the previous year. (These may not be paid in the coming year—something to check with your broker.)

b = In addition to the amount shown there was also a stock dividend. (There is no reason to assume any stock dividend or a similar one will be paid in the coming year.)

---

e = The amount indicated was paid in the last 52 weeks but there is no regular dividend rate.

g = Dividend shown is in Canadian currency.

j = The amount shown has been paid so far this 52-week period but the current dividend was suspended or not declared at the last board meeting. (Obviously not a good sign.)

Yield

The next column shows the percentage that the annual dividend constitutes of the current price. If the price of a security is $20 and the annual divided is $.50, then the annual yield is 2.5 percent. This is helpful only for investors considering a purchase of that security. If you already own the stock, that figure has nothing to do with the yield you are currently receiving. Your yield would depend on what you originally paid for the stock and the present dividend level.

P-E Ratio

This is the part of the newspaper quotation that is the most difficult to understand. It is also the most important. It provides a means of evaluating a security by relating a company's earnings to the price of its stock. It also allows you, with a little figuring, to determine the approximate earnings of a company, something not usually given in newspaper quotations.

The P-E ratio is the number of times the current price of

the stock exceeds the yearly per-share earnings of the company. That's powerful stuff; it's one of the first steps in coming to grips with the fundamentals of the company. Looking back at our example we see that the first stock, People's Energy Corporation (PeopEn) has a P-E ratio of 12. Looking farther along in the same line we see that the current price (the "Last" price) is 24⅝; which comes to $24.625 per share. If that figure is 12 times the per-share earnings of the company, then by dividing $24.625 by 12 we get $2.05 as the per-share earnings of People's Energy Corporation. We don't know how much the company made in total earnings because we don't have the number of shares outstanding, but however many there are, for every share the company earned about $2.05.

How is the P-E ratio useful? It gives us a concrete notion of what we are getting for our money. Buying a share of People's Energy is buying $2.05 worth of earning power. Even more important, it gives us a way to compare individual stocks with one another so long as they are within the same industry group.

Let's say we are considering buying stock in either People's Energy or Pep Boys, the next stock in the example. We look and see that Pep Boys has a P-E ratio of 22. (The "x" between the 22 and the 1545 simply means that the total number of round lots, 1,545, sold ex-dividend that day.) Since People's Energy has a P-E of almost half 22 it would seem that People's Energy is the better buy: its price is inflated less beyond the per-share earnings. But wait a minute. Pep Boys is a chain of retail stores and People's Energy is a utility. Utilities traditionally have a lower P-E ratio than retail stores. When we look elsewhere in the stock tables for utilities to compare with People's Energy, we see Connecticut Energy with a P-E of 14, Con Edison at 11, New

England Electric at 7.4, Texas Utilities at 8.6. Even from this superficial glance it looks like the average P-E of utilities is lower than for retail stores. It may be that People's Energy is even a little on the high side.

The P-E ratio can also help you compare companies of different sizes. If company A makes $10 million in profit and its stock sells for $5, and company B makes $100 million in profit and its stock sells for $50, how do you evaluate which is the better buy? The P-E ratio can help. If company A has 10 million shares outstanding, then the per-share earnings are $1 ($10,000,000 divided by 10,000,000 shares). If company B has 500,000,000 shares then the per-share earnings are $.20 ($100,000,000 dollars divided by 500,000,000 shares). So that while company B is a lot bigger, it also has a lot more dilution because of so many shares outstanding. Since the price of shares for both companies is $5, the P-E ratio of company A is 5 ($5/$1) and the P-E ratio of company B is 25 ($5/$.20).

What's a P-E Ratio?

The P-E ratio, short for price-earnings ratio, is the ratio of the current price of a stock to its per-share earnings. Stated another way, it's how many times the per-share price exceeds the per-share earnings. Even though the size of companies and the prices of their shares differ greatly their respective P-E ratios can give you a means for comparison. Comparisons are most meaningful between companies in the same business sector.

Sales—100s

This is the volume: how many round lots (100s) have been transacted. To the ordinary investor volume will not be meaningful, but any indication of increased trading should cause you to watch the news for a reason or to call your broker.

More meaningful to the average investor is the listing that most papers carry of the stocks that traded the most frequently during the previous day or week. These are called the "most active issues." The *Wall Street Journal* underlines the 20 most active stocks on both exchange listings (for issues selling for more than $5 a share and meeting certain other requirements). Other papers simply publish a list of the most actively traded.

High—Low—Close

The next three columns are generally price columns and report transaction prices only for the period of trading covered by the quotations. If it is a daily paper, the high will be the highest price paid the previous day, the low the lowest price paid, and the last will be the closing price for that day. A weekly paper will show the highs and lows for the entire week.

If you purchased a security, it is interesting to look at the next day's paper to see the price fluctuation for that security on the day you bought it. Did you buy it at the top or at the bottom?

The close is the final price paid during the previous

trading period. Most of the time, trading will open the next trading period at the same price although there are exceptions. If a stock is trading ex-dividend, that is, if the dividend payment was the previous day, then the price the following day will often open slightly lower. Often good or bad news after the market closes will also cause a stock to open at a different price the next day.

Net Change

This is the percentage change of the current closing price up or down from the closing price of the previous trading period. Watch this column for sudden price movement. Most papers also carry lists of the 10 or 20 biggest gainers and losers. If one of your securities appears on either of those lists and you don't know why—call your broker. The *Wall Street Journal* prints in boldface the quotation of any security that shows a net gain or loss of 5% or more from their previous closing price.

Stock Quotations

The most widely read source for stock and security quotations of all kinds is *The Wall Street Journal*. A guide to interpreting the *Journal*'s quotations is available with a subscription. It is entitled *The Wall Street Journal: Guide to Understanding Money & Markets*. It is also available from Prentice Hall Press for $12.95. (Prentice Hall Press, Englewood Cliffs, NJ 07632). The address of *The Wall Street Journal* is 200 Liberty Street, New York, NY 10281. A year's subscription is $139, six months is $71, 3 months is $37.

Another source is *The Investor's Guide to Stock Quotations* by Gerald Warfield available for $10.95 from Perennial Library (a division of HarperCollins) at Keystone Industrial Park, Scranton, PA 18512–1596. (800)242–7737.

SEVEN

Your Broker

A broker is an intermediary you must hire every time you want to buy or sell a security. The fees which the broker charges depend on the type of security and the size of the transaction. Brokerage fees reduce your profit or make your loss even more substantial.

Do you have to have a broker? Almost always, but here are a few cases where you don't:

1. A company you work for may offer its *own* stock to its employees. Usually this is through an automatic payroll deduction plan that purchases for you the same dollar amount of stock each pay period. Probably you will have many purchases so that the per-share price will end up being, over the long run, an average of all the prices you paid. That won't be the lowest price, but it won't be the highest, either. Since the fixed dollar amount deducted from your pay each period will seldom be the exact price of the stock or a multiple thereof, fractional amounts, for example 3.7 shares, will usually be included in your purchase. Sometimes a brokerage will be contracted by the company to administer such a plan and a fee will be charged.

2. Somebody you know owns some stock and they are willing to sell it to you directly. This is pretty rare, but it does happen. Most often it is in stock of companies that are not publicly traded which means, among other things, that there may be no current market price, and you will have to arrive at a price through negotiation.

How this works is that the owner signs the certificates over to you (there are blanks on the back of the certificates for this purpose). You then must return the certificate to the issuing company so that it can issue a new certificate with your name on it. Otherwise you are holding what is called a "dirty certificate," and you can't sell it in the same way you bought it because the blanks on the back of the certificate are filled. Besides, you want to be on record as the owner of the certificate by the company in order to receive the annual and quarterly reports, the proxy forms for the annual meeting, and the dividends, if any.

3. Here is a case where, although you have to use a broker, you don't have to pay a commission. That happens when brokerages sell an initial public offering. What this means is that the brokers are underwriters of the security: they are part of the sales team selling the stock for the issuing company, and they will sell you the stocks without a brokerage fee. (This is different from the usual transaction where the broker acts in your behalf to buy stock previously owned by a third party.) Such a procedure does not reflect on the soundness or lack of soundness of the security. It may be anything from a twenty-five cent stock to shares in a giant utility company. It means only that the shares are newly issued, either by a new company or an established company that is increasing its number of shares in circulation.

4. Once you own a stock, the company may offer to sell you more at the current market rate. Or, instead of receiving dividends in cash, some companies will let you roll over your earnings into extra shares.

The above instances, while not rare, are pretty limited ways to acquire stocks, which means that most of the time you'll have to pay a broker. So how do you keep brokerage fees down? The answer to that, surprisingly, is that you may not want to.

In seventeenth-century Amsterdam the owners of the Dutch East India Company could have increased the profit from their merchant ships by not hiring navigators to go along with their ships. After all, a navigator was one of the most expensive members of the crew. But none of the owners considered such an economy because they naturally feared for the safety of the boat without a navigator to chart its course. A possible alternative would have been for the owners to learn navigation and go along themselves.

For your investments you can put yourself in the hands of a broker or financial advisor, or you can go it alone, studying and making your own investment decisions. Probably the best is to do both: use a full-service broker, but participate in decisions yourself as much as possible.

Conventional wisdom has it that brokers are salespeople. That's not always true. Sometimes they are only clerks who perform tasks for hire: tasks you tell them to do. Those are discount brokers.

Deciding which broker to use is particularly difficult because you must do that first, before your initial transaction, before you've had any experience at all. If things don't work out you can always change brokers, but that would probably mean you've had an unpleasant experience, something you'd just as soon avoid.

Your decision as to whether to use a full-service broker or a discount broker will have bearing on all the other investment decisions you make, so we're going to take a hard look at brokers, what you can expect from them, and what you must expect from yourself.

The Full-Service Broker

Full-service brokers are an odd mixture of virtues and vices. Here are some of the virtues:

1. They offer you advice from their research department. Astute as your broker's intuition may be, the advice you want should be from the brokerage's research department. The person at the other end of the phone may be only a salesman. Although he or she may or may not have other qualifications they are probably not an analyst. Stock analysts have full-time, highly difficult jobs, and they don't deal with the public. What you want is for your broker (again, we are talking about the person who is talking to you on the phone) to pass along advice from the analysis department and to help you determine whether such an investment is appropriate for you.

2. A full-service broker should know your financial

circumstances and your investment objectives, and this should affect the type of investment he or she suggests to you. The investment objectives for a woman of 25 are different from a man of 50, or a single parent, or a hotshot lawyer, or a grandmother.

Should everyone look to discover a future IBM selling for 50 cents a share that will grow into a $100 a share? No. The investment strategy necessary to come up with such a security would involve buying a large number of penny stocks on speculation with no guarantee that you have found the winner you're looking for. It would be a portfolio of the highest risk and instability. It is the job of the full-service broker to determine the level of risk appropriate for your investment needs and to steer your portfolio accordingly.

3. You can establish a two-way relationship with a broker. They can understand what's going on in your life, and you can learn how to evaluate and interpret their offerings and advice.

Those were the virtues. Here are some of the vices.

1. Full-service stock brokers are salespeople. If they are established at the brokerage, then they are working on commission. They make money only when they induce you into making a transaction, either a purchase or a sale. Worst, the higher the risk of the security they sell you—the *higher* their commission.

That's not to say that they are paid precisely according to the riskiness of the stock. But certain over-the-counter stocks will carry a higher commission and certain non-stock investments like tax shelters will carry enormous commissions.

2. Similarly, once you've bought a stock, the broker

makes no further money on you until you do something else besides letting it sit there and grow. Many brokers don't want to be the guys who sold you the IBM 30 years ago at 50 cents a share. They want to be the salesfolk who've persuaded you to sell and buy other stocks every year or so thereafter generating continued commissions.

3. All customers are not equal in his/her eyes. Brokers will not usually watch the portfolio of a small investor and call with the latest news, warning, advice, etc. Of course that's a double-edged sword. You may not want him bothering you to induce you to frequent transactions. Nevertheless, many investors think their broker is watching their securities, but depending on the house rules of your brokerage, that may not be so.

The crux of the matter is that there is built into the structure of the broker/client relationship a conflict of interest. That needn't be so. For instance, European brokerage houses, in addition to brokerage fees, charge a small safe-keeping fee that takes the pressure off the broker to churn the account, that is, to propose needless buying and selling primarily for the purpose of generating commissions. Some brokerages have already initiated such fees, but only for special accounts like IRAs that are not expected to move much.

And finally, about your full-service broker, don't mistake him or her for a financial psychic. They receive good information which they can pass along to you, but they are not analysts. If they say they want to "check with someone" before answering one of your questions respect the fact that they are trying to get for you the best information available. Pay attention also to the advisory letter that the brokerage puts out. Often this is more valuable than the investment letters many subscribe to. It's usually written by the best minds at the firm.

Another thing to remember: since brokers' commissions are a cost of investing, they are tax deductible.

TYPES OF BROKER ORDERS

At the market: execute the order to buy or sell immediately at the lowest ask price or the highest bid price available. Also called a "market" order. This is the most common type of order.

Buy limit order: Do not pay more than a specified price for the security ordered.

Sell limit order: Do not sell for less than a specified price.

Buy-Stop order: Buy if the price rises to a specified level. This protects an investor who has sold short and must eventually buy a security to cover a short position.

Sell-Stop order: Sell if the price falls to a specified level.

The Discount Broker

So let's take a look at the alternative. With an account at a discount brokerage you won't always get the same person on the phone, and the person you do get won't know any more about you than what your account shows on their screen. Also, they won't give you any investment suggestions. Nevertheless, *you* are in charge. The transactions are swift and the fees are sometimes as much as 75% lower than a full-service broker.

What you have to decide is whether saving on the brokerage fee is more important than the work you have to put in staying up with your securities. You will have no advisor, no one to talk to—or will you?

How about advisory letters? If you decide on a discount broker you should probably subscribe to one or more investment letters or at least stay up with securities and the markets in the newspaper. *The Wall Street Journal* is the most universally available but there are a number of others including *Barron's,* a weekly, and the *Investor's Daily,* which contains comprehensive quotations and one-year-price charts for many securities. Of course, the cost of these publications eats up the savings on brokerage fees, which brings up an important point. The primary reason for choosing a discount broker should be because you are independent-minded, informed investor. Do not decide to use a discount broker solely because you want to save on commissions. If you aren't prepared to do your own investing you could make some very costly mistakes.

Keeping Your Commissions Down

All the former having been said, here are several things you can do to keep commissions down:

1. Don't buy odd lots, always buy in 100-share lots, called "round lots." Currently at a major full-service broker-age you will pay a 2.61% commission for 100 shares of AT&T while an odd lot will incur a 3.6% commission.

2. Use a discount broker when you are confident in what you are doing.

3. Be aware that the commission on large orders can be discounted. Discounts kick in at different "break points," for example, there are shares of mutual funds sold by most major brokerages on which the commission is 5.5% on purchases below $25,000, 5.25% on purchases above $25,000, and 4.75% on purchases above $100,000. If you are spreading money among several different funds try to invest above the "break point" in each fund you select rather than spreading your money out so thinly that you pay the highest rate for every investment.

4. Purchase mutual funds that have no commission. These are called "no-load" funds.

5. Avoid those over-the-counter stocks and thinly traded issues (i.e., not traded very often) that have higher commission rates.

6. Never be afraid to ask a broker how much the commission will be. Don't wait until you've already agreed on a purchase to see what the total will be after the broker "figures in" the commission.

7. If a broker tells you there is no commission find out how much the markup is. The markup is the difference between the price the brokerage pays for a security and the price they charge you. Don't confuse this with the "spread" between bid and asked price.

Danger Signs

Here are some signs that should make you worry. Consider changing firms if your broker:

1. only tries to sell you securities in which his own firm is a market maker. True, there's no commission, but this guy is pushing product.

2. tells you frequently that you have to "act now" on his investment tip. He's pressuring you.

3. suggests that you inflate your net worth on the account application. If something goes seriously wrong you have seriously weakened any case you might have against the brokerage.

4. proposes mostly investment products that have the highest commission such as limited partnerships, unit investment trusts, penny stocks, options, in-house mutual funds, and new issues.

Dispute With Your Broker?

If you feel your broker has managed your account poorly or misrepresented securities, you should complain to the branch manager of the broker's office. If you do not receive satisfaction, write to the NASD for their booklet, *Arbitration Procedures*, which will help you *and* your attorney in determining if you have a case for arbitration. The address is National Association of Securities Dealers, Inc., 2 World Trade Center, 98th Floor, New York, NY 10048. (212) 839–6251.

If you decide to file suit, write to the Director of Arbitration at the NASD (same address) or to the exchange on which your trades were executed for the necessary forms. For the NYSE that's Director of Arbitration, New York Stock Exchange, Inc., 11 Wall Street, New York, NY 10005. Claims of less than $10,000 can be handled by mail.

Do you have a chance? In 1990, 54% of the 1,530 cases heard by the NASD were won by the investors.

EIGHT

New Issues

The primary market and the secondary market are basic divisions within any securities market. The primary market is made up of the sale of new issues; the secondary market is for shares already in public hands. Stock exchanges are set up almost exclusively for the secondary market. New issues, on the other hand, trade over-the-counter.

You may have seen advertisements in the newspaper for new issues. Because it is illegal to sell shares of new issues without the buyer being in receipt of a prospectus, the ads for new issues give only bare, scant information. In fact, with their traditional black borders and oversized type these drab ads have come to be known as **tombstones.**

Going Public

When a company issues stock for sale to the general public for the first time that company is said to be "going public." It is likely that the company was **privately held** before, and the shares were in the possession of relatively few investors. Now the company is making a major bid for more capital and for public ownership. It has entered into an agreement with the brokers who will handle the public sale of its stock, the underwriters, and it is letting itself in for many more rules and regulations as it comes under all the restraints and requirements of the Securities and Exchange Commission (SEC) for publicly traded stock. Even though corporations are chartered through the states, the federal government now assumes regulatory power because the shares are being sold across state lines. Among the requirements are the filing of annual and quarterly reports with the SEC. Further SEC and NASD rulings require the timely publishing and availability of this information for investors.

If your broker suggests a new issue to you then you can be certain that your brokerage firm is an underwriter. No commission is charged on new issues, and so the brokerage makes its money by its underwriting fees. Under these circumstances your broker is not an impartial advisor but a salesman. Weigh the advice accordingly.

In the case of **hot issues** (where the price is expected to increase as soon as the shares start trading on the secondary market) there is a situation where your broker can do you a real favor. Often the shares available are apportioned to brokers who may receive enough only to offer them to a few customers. If indeed your broker offers you a hot issue it is a sign of regard; you are a most-favored customer.

Requirements of a Tombstone Ad

New issues and secondary offerings are advertised in "tombstone" ads which contain:

1. a disclaimer stating that the ad is not to be construed as an offer to sell the stock and that a prospectus is available.
2. The date of the offering.
3. The total number of shares being offered; sometimes the offering will be for units containing shares and warrants.
4. the par value which has evolved to be a meaningless number for common stock, the amount on which the interest is paid for preferred stock, and the principal amount for a bond. Some stock is issued with no par value.
5. The price of the shares or units
6. The list of underwriters from which you can get a prospectus and purchase the stock

---

Secondary Offering

A secondary offering is the sale of stock of a corporation that is already in existence. It may be a large block of stock owned by an individual, such as a founder of the corporation, or it may be a sale of stock from the corporation's store of unissued shares, called treasury stock. It may also be from a corporation that has recently amended its certificate of incorporation so as to issue a greater number of shares.

When a secondary offering is from the issuing corporation then that corporation receives money from the sale, if from some other source then the corporation receives none. It is mandatory, when the company issues additional shares to notify current shareholders so that they may purchase additional stock, proportional to the number they already own. The point is to allow the current shareholders to maintain their same degree of "stake" in the corporation. For example, if a corporation with two million shares outstanding decides to issue another million all its shareholders will be given the opportunity to purchase half again as many shares as they already own. This is of importance to the small shareholder because the purchase price to current shareholders may be substantially below the current market price.

Secondary offerings are handled similarly to new issues. A group of underwriters sell the stock to investors charging an underwriting fee to the company but no commission to the individual investor. A prospectus is required, as with a new issue, and the tombstone advertisements are under the same restraints. The big difference for investors is that a secondary offering is of stock in a company that has already gone public. It has a track record. There is more information available and, for this reason, there is less risk. Traditionally, the price of a secondary offering is the closing price of the previous days' trading.

It is the law that you must have a prospectus in your possession before you purchase any new issue or secondary offering. In fact, a sale can be voided if you can demonstrate that you did not have a prospectus at the time the sale was made.

Because warnings are printed in red ink on the first

page, the prospectus has become known as a "red herring." Technically it is a preliminary prospectus, since the official one isn't issued until the security begins trading on the market. Usually you are purchasing a new issue from a broker before it officially comes out for delivery to your account on the first day of trading.

New Issues of Penny Stock

The most hazardous of all new issues are those of penny stock. Major brokerages usually won't handle them, and so they are brought out by a consortium of small brokerages who specialize in these highly risky securities. There was a time when their salespeople would call incessantly wanting you to triple your money with their invariably hot issues until the SEC imposed the "cold-call" restriction mentioned in chapter 4.

There is money in the new issues of penny stock, but only if you have sufficient diversity to offset the many losers you'll have, and only if you have a relationship with a broker who will give you preferential treatment with respect to hot issues. That means you must be a steady customer. For the most part this is speculating, not investing. Do it at your own risk.

Information About New Issues

The preliminary prospectus, or red herring, is the official source of information about new issues. There is often little else available. If the corporation was previously closely held then it wasn't required to issue public financial statements. A computerized database service does offer on-line service to individual investors. Contact the Securities Data Company, Inc., 62 William Street, New York, NY 10005, and enquire about individual use of the "New Issues of Corporate Securities" database. (212) 668–0840.

NINE

Takeovers
And Tender Offers

Few rumors have the power to raise investors' expectations *and* stock prices like the hint of a takeover. Some analysts, known as **risk arbitragers,** pour all their energies into spotting companies ripe for the plucking and then buy up those securities, or guide others into buying them, in hopes the company will soon be the target of a corporate raider. This type of speculation is not for the faint of heart nor the shallow of pocket. However, every investor should know the mechanics of takeovers and tender offers because even the most conservative may one day be in the middle of a corporate battle. Handled properly, the stock of a takeover target can make you quick and substantial profit.

Mergers

Let's consider the most benign of these operations first, the merger. Mergers are, in fact, a kind of mutual takeover accomplished with the cooperation of the boards of both companies. Concessions are worked out with respect to the name of the new company, officers, assets, what plant stays open, what closes down, etc. Usually a price is agreed upon by which one company acquires sufficient stock in the other to control it. Once this is accomplished the target company may simply be absorbed into the parent company and the rest of its stock bought out or it may continue to live, even with the same name and management much as it did before the merger. This is a practical recourse because it makes the company a convenient package to sell at a later date should the merger prove not to be as profitable as expected.

Even in the most peaceful mergers, the price the takeover company is willing to pay is sometimes well above current market price, so you would be in for a windfall profit (assuming you didn't purchase the stock long ago when it was worth more). The price paid for the target company's stock may be in cash, stock of the parent company, or both.

Hostile Takeovers

There is no line at all between mergers and takeovers. They are varying degrees of the same thing, but when a merger meets sufficient resistance it is characterized as a hostile takeover. Sometimes the board of the company being acquired feels that the price being offered is too low, or perhaps they simply don't want to be acquired (especially if all the board and upper management stand to lose their jobs). Frequently, the two sides will air their views in the press, taking out ads to explain why their offer or point of view is reasonable and the other side's isn't. These public battles can result in the offering price being raised enough so that all parties are satisfied.

When no agreement can be reached, the aggressor company usually makes a tender offer to the shareholders at large, hoping to buy enough stock to wrest control from the board of directors. By law, these offers must be publicly advertised.

The amount of stock necessary to control a corporation can be far less than 50% depending on how widely disbursed the stock is, what the state regulations are, and how the articles of the company's certificate of incorporation read.

If you receive an offer to buy your stock, called a tender offer, you should consult your broker (more likely, your broker will be consulting you). If the offer is attractive, then there may be reason to act quickly. Some tender offers are for only a stipulated number of shares and there may be more shares tendered than wanted. This is called being "oversubscribed." Investors offering their shares after the quota has been filled will be turned away, or sometimes purchases are offered on a pro-rata basis. Also, there are time limits on tender offers so that stock may be tendered only for a limited time.

When a tender offer has been announced the price of the target company always jumps. It won't jump all the way to the level of the tender offer because there is still some chance the takeover will fail and the price of the stock will drop back to its pre-offer level.

Sometimes the situation gets really sticky (and profitable) when a second tender offer is made at a higher price by yet another company. If that happens the second company will provide you with forms so that even if you have already tendered your stock to the first company you may revoke that offer (if the deadline hasn't passed) and offer it instead to the second company.

The Language of Takeovers:

Tender offer–the public offer to buy the shares of a target company. A price and a time limit are always stipulated.

Hostile takeover–an attempt to force a merger on an unwilling corporation.

Proxy battle–a public attempt by an aggressor corporation to gain the votes of shareholders in a target company. No shares change hands at this stage although the eventual goal of the proxy battle may be to agree to a takeover.

Should You Join the Battle?

By the time the public hears of a tender offer there has already been a good deal of price movement in the stock. Even if you are watching the news closely, don't forget that the prices reported from the exchanges are always delayed by 15 minutes. A lot can happen on the floor of the New York Stock Exchange in 15 minutes.

Many investors buy in anyway. They figure that if the takeover goes through, the stock will rise to the level of the tender offer, or perhaps there will be a higher offer. That is not advisable unless you have expert advice. Prices that have risen sharply can fall just as rapidly, and you could be in the position of buying high and taking an immediate loss, whether on paper or in fact.

Investors sometimes find themselves on the other side of the fence, that is, holding stock in the aggressor company. If the view of the investing public is that the takeover is not good for the corporation (the company may have to take on an inordinate amount of debt to effect the takeover) then the price of your stock could fall, although it seldom falls substantially. A company in the position to take over another usually starts out, at least, in a strong financial position.

What Can Go Wrong?

There are many ways you can fail to make money in a takeover. If you bought the stock after the price had already gone up—the most dangerous way to play the game—you may be along for the ride down. If you already owned stock in the target company and tendered it, the offer may be oversubscribed. On the other hand, if an insufficient amount of stock was tendered then the whole thing could be off, and the price of your stock will fall.

The target company may also be able to fend off the acquisition. One of the worst-case scenarios is when the target company buys back at inflated prices the shares the aggressor company acquired so that now the corporation is in worse shape than it was before the takeover attempt.

Proxy Battles

When the board of a corporation resists a takeover sometimes
a proxy fight can ensue. If you own stock in the target
company you will be asked to sign over your proxy to one
group or another who want the takeover to go through. You
will not be selling your shares in this kind of action, and so
you will not make any money yet, but control can be wrested
from the board in this fashion which could mean a merger or
a sale of the securities to the aggressor company.

Not all tender offers are harbingers of great price
movement. Sometimes a company will decide to repurchase
some of its own stock simply because it feels its stock is
undervalued or it feels there has been too much dilution of
equity through too many shares in the public hands. The offer
of a corporation to buy back its own shares is also a tender
offer.

Defensive Action Against a Takeover

Here are some of the things companies do when faced
with a hostile takeover:

Take a Poison Pill–measures are adopted by the board
to make the company less attractive such as issuing a
preferred stock with a high dividend that the aggressor
company, presumably a growth company, would not
want to pay.

Find a White Knight–sometimes a company can find a more suitable company with which to merge, and though they will still be taken over it can be done so under more favorable conditions.

Make Golden Parachutes–when executives are afraid of losing their jobs they sometimes grant themselves lucrative severance pay or stock allowances should the takeover go through.

Can You Spot a Takeover?

A number of things make a company attractive as a takeover target. Perhaps the most common is its assets, whether cash or land or markets or whatever. However, if a broker recommends a stock simply because some other quality makes it attractive as a takeover target, be cautious. The company should have additional strengths, because if it is *not* taken over the price could fall over the long term. The stock of a company suspected of being a takeover target is already shored up by that expectation, and if a takeover doesn't materialize, the speculators will be bailing out and the price will drop.

Sometimes unusual volume, especially on a Friday, can precede a takeover attempt. The aggressor company may, for example, be quietly buying up the stock of the target company to acquire as much of it as cheaply as possible. When a company has acquired 5 percent of the stock of another company it is required to file a form 13D with the SEC. The acquiring company can claim that the acquisition is for investment purposes, and usually does, but the acquiring company can also experience a sudden change of heart.

Spotting takeover targets is not easy. Don't bother writing companies for copies of their 13D filings because the takeover will have come and gone by the time you receive it. Many investment letters point out takeover targets, but the best and most immediate sources are financial dailies like the *Wall Street Journal* or *Investor's Daily*. Look for notices of recent 13D filings. Sometimes they are grouped together and published once a week.

If you know accounting and would like to do some digging on your own get a copy of a corporation's 10K report. It's like an annual report without all the pictures. (Sometimes it's even typewritten!) It presents the data bare-bones without the interpretations that characterize the annual report. Compare the 10K with the slicker annual report and you'll probably get a different picture of the corporation. It's there you are most likely to find hidden assets.

How Destructive Are Takeovers?

The 1980's saw considerable abuse of corporate takeovers. The corporate "raider" was glamorized in the media, and some corporations liquidated assets or took on extra debt solely to defend themselves from being taken over. It was argued that such companies needed to undergo such trimming simply to render them more economically efficient—yet the result was factory and store closings, loss of jobs, and additional corporate debt. Even the aggressor companies sometimes came out the losers, finding themselves saddled with high interest junk bonds which they had to issue in order to finance a takeover that was beyond their means. Irresponsible investment bankers encouraged these forays into debt for their own immediate profit.

The instant wealth that takeovers can create is a hard prize to resist, but the harsh realities of heavy corporate debt and the loss of company assets have caused the financial community to rethink the benefit of these excesses. Currently mergers and takeovers seem to be based on strategic alliances between companies that are in related or complementary businesses so that the merger serves some immediately obvious purpose.

Do Your Own Research

You can see 10k, 10q (quarterly reports), or 13D reports of any company at one of four document rooms maintained by the SEC. They are in Washington (450 5th Street, NW), New York (26 Federal Plaza), Chicago (219 South Dearborn Street, Room 1204), and Los Angeles (5757 Wilshire Boulevard, Suite 500 East). You can get hard copies of these reports *not* through the SEC which will take forever but from one of the document retrieval services set up to provide quick and efficient service. Here are two with 800 numbers: Bechtel Information Services (20 cents a page and up) at 800–231-DATA is in Gaithersburg, MD. Disclosure, Inc. (a complete 10K is $25) at 800–638–8241 is in Bethesda, MD.

The Dow and Other Market Averages

The overall health of any financial market is reflected in its price averages. Before averages and indexes came along, investors would simply scan the newspaper quotations to get a rough day-to-day idea of whether the market as a whole was going up or down. All that changed in 1896 when the *Wall Street Journal* initiated the Dow Jones Industrial Average. The brain child of Charles Dow, one of the founders of the Dow Jones Company, the average took the hourly prices of 12 industrial stocks and calculated the arithmetic mean at pre-set intervals throughout the day.

In the days before computers, calculating a 12-stock average was about all they could keep up with, especially after it started getting more complicated with stock splits, mergers, and the replacing of some corporations with others in the average. Charles Dow, who was one of the leading financial analysts and economists of his day, believed that the average he had initiated could signal the beginnings and ends of major market movements. Significantly, he never used the average to predict price movement for any one stock in the average.

Almost a hundred years later you would think the average would have evolved significantly, but instead it became frozen in time. Today it is made up of only 30 stocks, a shockingly narrow sample of one of the world's major stock exchanges. Perhaps the average resisted change because it was the first of its kind, perhaps it is because it always had a successful business publication behind it. Whatever the reason, the DJIA has changed little substantively. The formulas have been refined and corporations have come and gone from the lists, but essentially it's the same as when it was founded. Here are the companies which constitute the DJIA today:

**Stocks of the
Dow Jones Industrial Average**

Allied-Signal	Caterpillar	Exxon
Alcoa	Chevron	General Electric
American Express	CocaCola	General Motors
AT&T	Disney	Goodyear
Bethlehem Steel	Du Pont	IBM
Boeing	Eastman Kodak	International Paper

McDonald's	Philip Morris	Union Carbide
Merck	Proctor & Gamble	United Technologies
3M	Sears Roebuck	Westinghouse
Morgan JP	Texaco	Woolworth

The Dow Jones Company also tracks three other averages, a utilities average, a transportation average, and a composite average. The others do not enjoy the popularity of the Industrial Average.

Other Averages and Indexes.

Today, every exchange, every market, even investment services and newsletters have indexes and averages. Some are broadly based and cover every stock in their industry group, and some are selective. Of the widely-quoted indexes, the New York Stock Exchange has five (Composite, Industrial, Utilities, Transportation, Financial), NASDAQ has four (Industrial, Insurance, Banks, Composite), Standard & Poor's has six, and Value Line has two.

Most analysts are skeptical about what they can infer from an average that tracks only 30 issues, so they also follow other indexes. The most well-known after the DJIA is the NYSE Composite Index which incorporates every stock on the exchange. Founded in 1966, it provides a comprehensive measure of the change in aggregate market value of all NYSE stock adjusted to eliminate the effects of capitalization changes like stock splits, new listings and delistings. The market value of each stock is obtained by multiplying its price per share by the number of shares listed. The sum of the individual market values is then expressed as a relative of the base period market value. The base value was set at 50.00 because at the initiation of the Index that figure was reasonably close to the average price of all common stocks (figured per dollar value).

Importance of Market Averages

For the individual investor, the daily movement of the various stock averages is not terribly important so long as that movement stays within reasonable limits. To be sure, fortunes are made and lost on options and futures based on these indexes, but this is usually remote from the world of the individual investor. There are, however, two ways that the stock averages, particularly the DJIA, take on more immediacy. One way is as a measure to compare the market's rises and falls with other years. For example, on October 12, 1989, the Dow dropped 190.58 points. It was a Friday, the public was worried, and there was a whole weekend to evaluate and analyze. How bad was the drop, really? One of the major comforts was the fact that the drop on that Friday could be compared with the last major fall in the market. On October 19, 1987 (one week short of two years earlier) the largest drop in history had occurred: 508 points. The '89 drop was not half as bad, literally. And, in fact, the market recovered 88.12 of its lost points on Monday to close at 2657.38. Newspapers said it was "a sharp correction, but not a calamity." An interesting note to the story is that the NYSE actually lost money on that Monday. The rally, it turned out, was primarily in the blue chips, and you don't get bluer-chipped than the 30 stocks of the Dow Jones Industrial Average. At any rate, the DJIA said the market was recovering, and eventually it did.

Another case in which market indicators can be useful is to evaluate the progress of your own portfolio. It might be helpful if in your own record keeping you jot down the DJIA or other market average number on the dates of your brokerage statements. This way you have a handy parallel track with which you can compare your portfolio's performance to the rest of the market. If the 10 percent increase in the value of your portfolio occurred when the Dow was increasing by 20 percent, then you know your own portfolio has underperformed the market. Consistent performance like this would be grounds for considering a different broker, or advisory letter, or investment strategy.

Where Do You Get the Figures for Indexes and Averages?

All newspapers that carry stock quotations carry at least some indexes and averages. *The Wall Street Journal*, of course, carries the Dow Jones Averages and all the other major ones. For your record keeping (to compare your portfolio against a market index) all you have to record periodically is the number at which the index closed. For page-wide, nine-month graphs of the DJIA and the S&P 500 see the *Investor's Daily*. Small year graphs of many companies as well as half-page, three-year graphs of spotlighted companies are also featured.

ELEVEN

Bonds on the Stock Exchange

Other Things That Trade on Stock Exchanges

Although we use the name "stock" exchange, other financial instruments are traded there besides stock, some because they always were, like bonds, and some, like options and futures, because they didn't exist before, and a stock exchange is the logical place for them to trade. (The latter, however, also trade on their own exchanges.) A complete consideration of all these instruments is not possible here but bonds, as the primary investment alternative to stock, deserve discussion in any examination of the stock exchange.

Bonds

Bonds are loans. When you buy a bond you loan a company money (or a municipality, or a government agency, etc.) and that company agrees to pay you back *and* to make regular interest payments to you in the meantime. To state it a little more precisely, the issuing company must return to you the face value of the bond (usually $1,000) upon maturity. The company must also pay you interest at the stated rate, called the "**coupon rate**." Interest payments are bi-annual so that you will receive half the annual interest amount every six months.

One of the ways that a bond is different from a personal loan or a mortgage is that loan payments always include both interest and principal so that the principal is gradually paid back over the life of the loan. With a bond all the principal is repaid at maturity in one lump sum.

Since a bond is a debt obligation, bond interest is more secure than stock dividends. A corporation must pay interest on its loans (including bonds) whether it makes a profit that year or not.

Companies put out more issues of bonds than they do stock. A glance at a bond table might show seven or eight issues for AT&T bonds, but in the stock tables there is only one issue of common stock. You might see, for example, ATT 7s03 meaning an AT&T bond paying 7% interest (the coupon rate) maturing in the year 2003. The "s" in bond quotations is inserted only to separate numbers for purposes of clarity. Sometimes omitted, it does reflect the way the bonds are referred to by brokers. This bond, for example, would be called the "AT&T 7s of 03." The first two digits of the year are omitted for brevity.

The Parts of a Bond

The **face value** of a bond is the total amount to be repaid at maturity, also called the **principal amount** or the **par value**. The **coupon rate** is the amount of interest paid annually, and it never varies. The coupon rate is stated as a percentage and calculated from the face value, not from what you pay for the bond.

Bond Prices

The face value of a bond is what the issuer pays upon maturity. Most are $1,000, however, that is rarely what you will pay for a bond. For example, what if a bond paid 10 percent but the current interest rates were lower for other debt instruments of the same calibre—say 8 percent. Investors would be willing to pay more for a bond that yielded higher-than-current rates, but of course, in doing so they would be lowering the rate. If they were willing to pay up to $1,250 then an annual interest payment of $100 would be exactly 8 percent of what was paid for the bond, and you'd be back at the current interest rate. In this way the prices of bonds are adjusted so that the fixed interest payments approximate prevailing interest rates.

If it's so simple then why, you might ask, is there so much difference between the various prices of bonds? There are two other factors in bond pricing. The first is that on maturity you will receive only the face value of the bond, no matter what you paid for it. In the above case you paid $1,250 for the bond, but in 2003, when the bond matures, whoever owns it will receive only $1,000. This capital loss will, of course, affect the price of the bond so that an investor would pay less for it. In some cases you will purchase a bond at a price below face value so that at maturity you will have a capital gain. That will, of course, increase the price of the bond.

Another aspect of bond pricing is the rating of the bond issue. Two rating companies, Moody's and Standard & Poor's, rate bonds according to the financial stability of the issuing company, their ability to meet interest payments, and their ability to return the principal on maturity. Bonds with a high rating command a higher price—and thus pay a lower rate of interest—than a bond with a low rating. Besides your broker, the best place to get bond ratings is *The Investor's Daily* which gives the Standard and Poor's rating for exchange listed bonds.

Current Yield

The current yield is given in most bond quotations. It is the percent the annual interest will be of the current price listed in the quotation. If a 10 percent bond costs $1,250 then you know two things. Your annual interest payment will be $100 because the coupon rate is 10 percent and the face value of the bond is $1,000. And you also know that the $100 annual interest is 8 percent of the price you paid so that the current yield is 8 percent.

The Rest of the Quotation

Sometimes the volume of bond sales is given. Unlike stocks, the number given is the exact number of bonds sold (bonds do not trade in lots). It is hard for the ordinary investor to glean meaningful information from the volume unless it is completely out of line with the volume of other bonds of the same general grade. If you do notice heavy volume check also the current price, and if there is a substantial change you should call your broker for news.

The current price shown in newspaper quotations is the closing price of the last trading period. This is the amount on which the current yield is based. Sometimes a "change" column appears at the end which gives the change of the current closing price from the closing price of the previous trading period.

An important aspect of bond prices that most first-time investors don't realize is that when you buy a bond on the secondary market, that is, a bond that is not a new issue, then you must reimburse the former owner of that bond with the interest that has accrued to date. What happens is that the broker simply tacks on this interest to the price of the bond. However, this amount is made up to you because when the first interest payment comes it will be a check for the full amount, even if the purchase was made only last week. If you are selling a bond, then you will receive the accrued interest since the last six-month payment. Paying accrued interest to the former bond owner is a way of simplifying the bookkeeping of bond payments. Otherwise the issuer would have to send both the seller and the buyer a check at the next payment date proportioned according to how long each party had held the bond.

Buying Bonds

Bonds can be bought through stock brokers and held in brokerage accounts just like stock. Your statement will inform you of all interest payments just as it does of all dividends or other security transactions. Banks will also purchase and hold some bonds for you, particularly municipal and government bonds.

Bonds are a "fixed income" security because the interest payments are fixed and do not vary. They are generally safer than stocks because bonds have a prior claim on the assets of a corporation. If the corporation fails, then the bondholders will have their principal returned before the stockholders receive anything.

Other Features of Bonds

Convertible: Some bonds can be converted into the stock of the issuing company. In quotations you will see the abbreviation "cv" used to indicate this feature. Usually it appears in the yield column (instead of the yield) which is no loss of information since you can calculate the current yield by dividing the annual interest amount by the current price of the bond.

In deciding whether you want to convert a bond into common stock, you should consider factors such as the current value of the stock. If the market value of the total number of shares you could get for your bond was under

$1,000, then you would not want conversion since you would take an immediate capital loss. If it were greater, then you would have to decide whether you wanted the immediate capital gain as opposed to the loss of the regular interest payments.

In real life you would never convert a bond into common stock simply to realize a profit. It wouldn't be necessary. The price of a convertible bond would track the price of the securities into which it could be converted once that price exceeded the face value of the bond. In order to take a profit you would just sell the bond.

Yield to maturity: This is a figure that's hard to get except from your broker. The only one of the investment newspapers that gives it is *The Investor's Daily,* which prints the best bond quotes of any paper. This yield is extremely hard to calculate, but it attempts a more realistic picture of your yield because it figures in the number of years left until maturity and the capital gain or loss you will have when the principal is refunded to you. Yield to maturity is one of the best ways to compare the yield of bonds that have different amounts of time left until maturity, different coupon rates, and different amounts of capital gain or loss at the time of redemption.

Discount and Premium: These are terms you will hear when buying or selling bonds. A bond selling at premium is selling above face value while a bond selling at discount is selling below face value.

Bearer and registered bonds: Most bonds are registered in the name of the bondholder by the issuing company so that the interest payments can be mailed to you (or your broker). However, you can still purchase older bonds which have coupons attached to the bond certificate (called the debenture). Holders of bearer bonds have to "clip the coupons" and send them in to the issuing corporation (or municipality) in order to get the interest payment due. The benefit of coupons is anonymity (if you want anonymity), but clipping coupons is a bother. If you have bearer bonds your broker or bank will usually clip and mail your coupons for you.

Calling: The call feature of a bond allows the issuer to buy back the bond before maturity if it chooses to do so. Sometimes there are time limits, like after so many years, sometimes there is a penalty so that the company has to pay you a premium over the face value. Nevertheless, this is a danger for high coupon bonds. In periods of low interest rates corporations will be anxious to retire bonds on which they are paying a high rate of interest. Always check the call feature with your broker.

Floating rate bond: This is a bond whose coupon rate changes depending on some outside measure like the prime rate.

Zero coupon bond: This kind of bond does not pay interest until the bond matures, and then you get it all—principal and interest—in one lump sum. It's appropriate for some situations, but you have to pay tax at the coupon rate every year just as if you were receiving the cash. This will be helpful at maturity because most of the interest you will receive in that lump sum you will already have paid tax on.

Flat: A bond trading flat means that it trades without payment or accrued interest to the former owner. It is trading that way because it missed its last interest payment or it has already matured. This bond is in trouble or involved in a special situation. Stay away unless you know what you are doing.

Bonds and Interest Rates

The price of bonds is immediately effected by a change in interest rates. The most visible is the **prime rate** which is the rate banks give their most credit-worthy corporate customers. Although it receives the greatest attention in the media, the prime rate tends to be the last to move. Brokers trying to anticipate interest rates keep an eye on other rates and even futures such as 30-year Treasury Bill futures as an interest rate indicator.

There is a tendency for all interest rates to move more-or-less together, so that when one rate goes up all other interest rates tend to go up accordingly, such as the rate at which you might be able to get a mortgage. The crucial factor for bond prices is that the coupon rate of the bond always remains the same. If a bond has a 5 percent coupon rate it will pay the bondholder $50 per year in two $25-dollar payments no matter if the prime rate is 2 percent or 20 percent. If the coupon rate of a bond is higher than the prevailing rate for that level of bond then everyone will want it; they will pay more for it, and the law of supply and demand will keep the price rising until the yield more or less equals the current rate for that level of bond.

> ## Here are the name of some bonds as they would appear in bond quotations. Can you read them?
>
> IBM 9s98 = an IBM bond with a 9 percent coupon rate maturing in 1998. It pays $90 interest annually in two $45 payments, one every six months. To figure your current yield divide $90 by what you paid for the bond.
>
> IBM 7½11 = an IBM bond with a 7½ percent coupon rate maturing in 2011. It pays $75 interest annually in two $37.50 payments, one every six months. To figure your current yield divide $75 by what you paid for the bond.

Bonds on the New York Exchange

Over 300 separate issues of bonds are traded on the New York Stock Exchange. Since the mechanics of bond trading are so different from that of stocks, bond trading has tended to be separate from other security transactions and is now in a completely different room on a lower floor of the stock exchange building. The computer support for these trades is fully as complex as for stock trading, and a separate bond ticker is maintained.

The size of the bond market is enormous, several times that of stocks, which is a surprise to most people. For small investors there is a rule that the purchase of nine bonds or less must go to the trading floor (they cannot be transacted by computer) which is just the opposite of the way stocks are handled.

Bonds and Your Broker

If you plan to invest primarily in bonds, then you may want a broker who specializes in bonds. Most registered representatives deal primarily in stock so you should check with the manager of the brokerage to see that you are assigned to an appropriate broker.

Things to Ask When You Buy a Bond

1. What is the rating by Moody's or Standard & Poor's?
2. What is the yield to maturity? Don't forget that's different from the current yield and is a helpful way to compare different bonds.
3. Is it callable? What are the chances of it being jerked out from under you by the issuing company?

The Best Source for Bond Quotations

The best bond quotations in an investment newspaper are those in *The Investor's Daily*. Both the S&P rating for the bond and the yield to maturity is given *in addition* to the current yield. Remember, however, that only bonds listed on the NYSE or AMEX are quoted. Newsstand price is $.50. One-year subscription is $149, six months is $79. Subscription address is 1941 Armacost Ave., Los Angeles, CA 90025 or call (213) 477-1453.

TWELVE

A Bit Of History

Knowing something of the history of the stock exchange and the instruments that trade on these exchanges will not help you with every-day investment decisions, but having some idea of the background and traditions of the securities markets will help you appreciate the exchanges, their products, and the economic system within which it is necessary for them to function. It will also give you an inkling of what other countries are going through or will soon go through that have recently turned to capitalism.

The New York Stock Exchange dates back to 1792 when twenty-four businessmen, merchants mostly, decided to meet every day for the purpose of buying and selling stocks and bonds. More of a broker's union than a stock exchange, the group gathered at the site that's now 68 Wall Street beneath a large buttonwood tree. (For you Southerners, like me, that's a cottonwood tree.) Mostly they traded government bonds that had been issued in 1789 to finance the Revolutionary Wars debt, and shares of the newly-formed Bank of the United States, and the stocks of various other banks and insurance companies.

Securities at this time were traded by commodity auctioneers in street auctions in front of 22 Wall Street along with bales of cotton and barrels of sugar. In fact, it was dissatisfaction with the auctions and the after-auction undercutting engaged in by some traders that caused these men to sign what has come to be known as the Buttonwood Agreement whereby they agreed to "avoid public auctions," charge a minimum commission, and "give preference to each other" in all their transactions.

Stock exchanges had already existed in Europe for over 200 years (London, Paris, and Amsterdam being the major ones), so that what these men did was hardly new, but it marked a definite step in the maturation of a country whose constitution was only five years old and whose first president was in his first term of office.

Two years earlier the first U.S. stock exchange had been formed in Philadelphia, but it could never compete successfully with the New York exchange. At this time two-thirds of all imports arrived through New York harbor. New York was even the nation's capital, George Washington having been sworn into office three years earlier at Federal Hall, across the street from where the New York Stock Exchange now stands.

After a year the fledgling exchange moved indoors into the Tontine Coffee House, also on Wall Street. Later, the men rented a room at 40 Wall Street. New members were added at this time by vote of the current members who placed a white ball or a black ball in a box. Too many black balls and a member was rejected. New rules of order were adopted like a twenty-five cent fine for not wearing a hat or for interrupting the president.

How did trading take place? It was a roll call system. The list of securities was read out two or three times a day, and when a security's name was announced, those who wanted to buy or sell shouted out their orders.

What qualified as capital stock was loosely defined, and there were substantial differences in incorporation requirements from state to state. In 1855 the English Parliament granted limited liability to private investors who held corporate stock, a right absolutely fundamental to the corporate system. This and other reforms were gradually adopted in the U.S. along with more uniformity among the state incorporation laws. By the mid-nineteenth century the exchanges began to impose regulations on the corporations it listed, such as the requirement that corporations divulge how many shares they had outstanding.

The number of private investors in the U.S. remained small through most of the nineteenth century partly because brokers would only accept orders from well-established, wealthy individuals. But by 1886 a million shares were traded on the New York Stock Exchange for the first time, and speculation in the stock market changed from an activity exclusively indulged in by the wealthy to something akin to a sporting event. Everyone could participate. Stocks were purchased on margin (credit) with as little as 10 to 15 percent down by people who could never afford the full price. No one minded, because the value of stocks was only expected to rise. The strategy was that the stock could be sold at any time in the future for a higher price. If this happened before the investor had paid for the stock—and it usually did—the investor could pay back the broker the amount borrowed on the original purchase and still come out with a profit.

To appreciate fully the stock market crash of 1929 we need to go a little deeper into margin purchases. When stock is bought on margin, the amount advanced to the investor by the broker (to enable the investor to pay cash for the stock) is considered a secured loan. The stock itself is the collateral for the loan, and the broker always holds that stock in a special account (a margin account) for the investor. If the investor doesn't pay the loan back in a reasonable amount of time, then the broker who holds the security has the option of foreclosing. In such a case, the broker would immediately sell the stock, reimbursing the firm for the loan plus interest, and the investor would be entitled to whatever was left over after costs.

But when the value of stock that has been purchased on margin drops substantially, the loan is no longer fully collateralized, since the stock isn't worth as much as it was. This causes the broker to go back to the investor and demand that he or she put up more money to cover the amount that the stock has fallen in value, that is, to deposit additional collateral. This is known as a margin call.

From 1921 to 1929 the number of new stock issues created to feed the growing appetite for securities rose from 1,800 to 6,500. Often these companies were underfinanced. Unfortunately, the underwriters of new issues were banks, and the banks used their depositors' money to invest heavily in the stocks of companies they were bringing out. In short, the banks speculated with their depositors' money.

On October 24, "Black Thursday," the market experienced a sharp drop in heavy trading. Everyone from President Herbert Hoover to the local bank president assured the public that the market would rally, but on Tuesday, October 29, 1929 the market crashed. A record 16,000,000 shares were traded in a frenzy of selling. Margin calls went out all over the country to people who didn't have the money to pay for their securities or, if they did, their money was in a bank that had just failed. The ticker tape of the day, which printed only 285 characters a minute, was unable to keep up with the heavy volume, lagging behind trading by almost two hours, so that even brokers did not know how bad it was. In the following weeks, trading was curtailed and brokers tried to sort out their accounts. A small rally appeared and failed. A consortium of bankers raised a billion dollars to help shore up prices, but to no avail.

By 1932, the Dow Jones Industrial Average had dropped from 386 to 41. Individual issues did even worse. RCA dropped from 115 to 3, General Motors from 97 to 7.

Fundamental economic problems were at the root of the stock market crash and the ensuing Great Depression, and these problems were exemplified in many of the business practices of the day such as the speculation by banks in the stock market and insufficient margin requirements for investors. Six thousand banks failed during this time and hundreds of thousands of investors lost their life savings.

To an extent our modern securities market was shaped in response to the crash of '29. Congress, in desperation, passed three major pieces of legislation designed to correct the abuses of the past and assure that specific unsound business practices would not contribute to such a debacle again. The first was the Glass-Steagall Act of 1933 which prohibited banks from underwriting securities. Thus we have in this country a separation of banks and brokerages which does not exist in most other countries. The Federal Deposit Insurance Corporation was also created to protect the deposits of the public. The second piece of legislation was the Securities Act of 1933 which required that new issues of stock be registered with the Federal Trade Commission and that all information concerning these new issues be made available to the public through a prospectus. The third was the Securities Exchange Act of 1934 which created the Securities and Exchange Commission to enforce these regulations.

Regulation, of course, can't guarantee a healthy market, and in any case, there will always be corrections as well as major movements up and down. On October 19, 1987, the second crash of the century occurred when the Dow Jones Industrial Average plummeted 508 points for a 22.6 percent loss.

Over the years, the fine-tuning of the market place by laws, regulations, and enforcement has made it one of the fairest, most efficient markets in the world. This isn't the case in every country. On the Tokyo exchange, for instance, where regulations are vague and enforcement lax, there has never been a single conviction for insider trading. Recent abuses by Japanese brokerage funds have brought apologies, but no reforms.

On the New York Stock Exchange, current problems include wide swings in prices brought about by large-scale computerized trading. Rules restricting this and other types of mechanized trading have been put into place, but probably further steps will be needed. Another issue facing the exchange is the buying up of specialist firms (the market makers) by large brokerages. And for the future, studies are under way to better adapt exchange trading to the world trading of securities, specifically, how will the New York Stock Exchange fit into a global market of 24-hour per day trading. Certainly we can be sure that the New York Stock

Exchange and the other U.S. exchanges will continue to grow and adapt to the emerging world stock market.

Firsts on the
New York Stock Exchange:

Here are some of the milestones in the development of the New York Stock Exchange.

May 17, 1792 Bottonwood agreement signed by 24 businessmen who met regularly under a tree at 68 Wall Street to trade securities.

?, 1793 Newly formed exchange begins to meet in the Tontine Coffee House.

March 8, 1817 Organization of brokers established, a constitution and name, "New York Stock & Exchange Board."

March 16, 1830 Smallest number of trades ever made: only 31 shares traded.

January 29, 1863 Name changed to New York Stock Exchange.

November 15, 1867 First stock ticker introduced.

December 15, 1886 First day one million shares traded.

January 23, 1895 The exchange first recommended that listed companies publish their annual statements, including an income statement and a balance sheet.

July 31 to December 11, 1914 Longest closing of the exchange, almost five months, because of World War I.

October 29, 1929 Stock market crash: 16,410,000 shares traded in frantic selling.

June 4, 1952 First member of the exchange to be a corporation.

February 18, 1971 New York Stock Exchange incorporated as a not-for-profit corporation.

April 30, 1975 Fixed commissions abolished.

March 1, 1976 Computerized system for execution of small orders completed, the DOT System (Designated Order Turnaround)

February 3, 1977 Membership in exchange opened to foreign brokerages.

August 18, 1982 First day 100 million shares traded.

September 21, 1987 Highest price ever paid for a seat on the exchange: $1,150,000.

October 19, 1987 Second crash of the century. Largest point drop in the Dow Jones Industrial Average in history: 508 points.

October 20, 1987 Highest volume record: 608,148,710 shares.

More Information on the Stock Market

The *Fact Book* published every year by the New York Stock Exchange contains a summary of the year's activity and various statistical data updated yearly. Current price is $10.00 and may be obtained by writing the New York Stock Exchange, Inc., Publications Department, 11 Wall Street, New York, N.Y. 10005, or by calling (212) 656–5273.

Marketplace: A Brief History of the New York Stock Exchange, published by the New York Stock Exchange, chronicles the history of the exchange from its beginnings to today's modern computerized trading environment. It also highlights the NYSE's role in the financial and industrial development of the nation. Price is $5.95.

Glossary

account executive *See* "registered representative."

American depository receipt (ADR) A certificate representing foreign securities that facilitates their trading in this country. These certificates are traded in lieu of the original certificates which remain on deposit with an American bank in the country of origin.

American Stock Exchange (ASE or AMEX) Formerly known as the "curb exchange" because it originated as an outdoor market where securities were traded on the street. It is located on the other side of Trinity Church from the New York Stock Exchange.

AMEX The American Stock Exchange.

Annual report A financial statement issued each year by all public corporations. Required by the SEC, these reports are sent to all shareholders and should present a comprehensive picture of the financial health of the corporation.

arbitrage The simultaneous purchase and sale of the same security on different markets or exchanges. The purpose is to net a small but instant profit for the arbitrageur by taking advantage of price discrepancies that sometimes appear for the same security on different markets.

ASE The American Stock Exchange.

ask price The price at which a broker is willing to sell a security to you. This price will be higher than the bid price. For over-the-counter securities, the bid and ask prices are often both quoted.

as principal This is when a broker sells you a security from its own account. Often the broker will be a market maker or an underwriter of the security. There is no brokerage fee when a broker sells a security as principal, although there will be a markup on the ask price.

at-the-market A type of order when a broker is asked to buy or sell immediately at the best possible price. Also known a "market order." This is the most common type of security transaction.

average down The purchase of additional shares after the price of the shares has dropped. The average price paid for all the shares will be between the two purchase prices thus averaging down the cost of the initial transaction.

bear An investor who anticipates a drop in security prices and invests accordingly.

bid price The price at which a broker is willing to buy a security from you. This will be lower than the ask price. For over-the-counter stocks both the bid and ask price are often quoted in the newspapers.

big board The New York Stock Exchange, so named for the large quote boards once used in the main trading room to post bid and ask prices.

blue sky laws State laws protecting investors from fraud and misrepresentation in the marketing and sale of new securities. The story is that once a judge, commenting on a particular stock, said that it had about as much value as a patch of blue sky.

book value The per-share net worth of a stock obtained by subtracting the liabilities of a corporation from its assets and dividing by the shares outstanding. Liquidation value of preferred stock must also be deducted. Sometimes called stockholder's equity.

broker The usual term for a registered representative in a brokerage firm: an individual who handles customer accounts. In fact, a broker is an individual licensed to execute public orders in securities.

brokerage A firm licensed to execute public orders for securities. *See also* "commission."

bucket shop A brokerage which defrauds the public by any number of illegal practices and or by specializing in questionable new issues, especially penny stock.

bull An investor who anticipates a rise in security prices and who invests accordingly.

capital gain The net profit from a securities transaction after deducting any commissions or other costs.

capital stock *See* "common stock."

churning The unnecessary buying or selling of securities within an account in order to generate commission fees for the broker.

class Distinguishes some issues of stock from other issues of the same company. For instance, a corporation might issue three classes of preferred stock each with a different dividend rate. These would usually be labeled as class A, class B, class C, etc.

closing price The last price at which a security transaction took place for a specific security during a specific trading period. Usually the last price quoted in newspaper stock tables.

commission The fee charged an investor by a brokerage firm for the handling of a security transaction. Also known as the *brokerage*.

common stock A unit of equity ownership in a corporation. Also known as *capital stock*. Distinguished from preferred stock by the latter's (usually) guaranteed dividend, or lack of voting rights, or prior claim to the assets of the corporation in case of bankruptcy.

consolidated tape The ticker tape. Network A is for issues listed on the New York Stock Exchange, and network B is for the American Stock Exchange. Quotations are broadcast to quote terminals, ticker displays, and cable television only after a fifteen minute delay, giving brokers trading on the exchange first chance to react to price changes.

cornering the market Control of enough of one security or commodity to permit price manipulation.

corporation The predominant form of business in free-market economies. Owners (stockholders) separate from management. In a closed corporation, shares are held by relatively few individuals, whereas in a public corporation, the shares are traded publicly on an exchange or over-the-counter. Shareholders are not liable for the indebtedness of the corporation, a concept known as *limited liability*.

cumulative (preferred) stock A sometime feature of preferred stock where past dividends, if missed, must be paid at a later date. Payment of cumulative dividends takes precedence over the payment of common stock dividends.

current yield For stocks, this is the percent of the purchase price returned by the annual dividend.

CUSIP number An identification number on stock and other security certificates. Abbreviation is for the Committee on Uniform Security Identification Procedure. Every security certificate has a unique CUSIP number.

date of record Last day on which you can buy a stock and still get the current dividend. The security is sold ex-dividend the following day, at a price reduced by the amount of the dividend.

Designated Order Turnaround (DOT) The computerized system for processing small securities transactions by computer at the specialist's station.

dividend An amount declared by the board of directors to be distributed among shareholders on a per share basis. In the U.S., dividends are usually paid in quarterly payments although they appear in newspaper quotations as annual amounts. Usually dividends are paid from a corporation's profits so that dividends tend to rise when a company's profits rise. Sometimes dividends are in the form of additional stock. For preferred stock the dividend is fixed and does not normally change.

dollar cost averaging The regular purchase of a fixed dollar amount of stock over the long term. The usual form of dollar cost averaging is through payroll deduction plans. The price paid for the stock will, of course, end up being the average of all the prices paid.

DOT *See* "designated order turnaround."

Dow-Jones averages Market averages for different industry groups initiated by the *Wall Street Journal*. The most famous, the Dow-Jones Industrial Average, is made up of thirty industrial stocks. The average is calculated by taking the closing price for each security and dividing it by a divisor that compensates for any inequities such as past stock splits.

down tick A security transaction that takes place at a price below that of the previous transaction.

earnings The net profit of a corporation. Sometimes reported as per-share earnings. It is usual for earnings reports in the newspapers to compare the current earnings of a corporation (for the quarter, yearly, etc.) with the same period of a year ago.

equity Ownership. Usually that amount of ownership which is cleared after deducting any liabilities.

ex-distribution The first day a security trades without the current dividend.

ex-dividend The first day a security trades without the current dividend. If the stock had been purchased the previous day the purchaser would have received the current dividend.

ex-rights or **ex-warrants** The first day a security trades without its rights or warrants. Frequently, new issues trade in units which include one share and any number of rights or warrants. In this case the rights or warrants have expired.

fully diluted earnings per share A per-share earnings figure that assumes all convertible securities (preferred stocks or bonds) have been exchanged for common stock.

fundamental analysis A broad-based study of a corporation and its securities based on a detailed examination of its financial report, its management, and the sector of the market in which it operates. Usually contrasted with *technical analysis*.

growth stock Stocks considered likely to appreciate in value faster than the stocks of other corporations in the same market sector. Growth stocks usually pay low dividends or none at all.

holder of record The investor owning a security on the day the dividend is distributed. This is the day before the stock trades *ex-dividend*.

hot issue A new issue of stock expected to increase in price as soon as the issue is sold out and it begins trading on the secondary market, that is, on an exchange or over-the-counter.

initial distribution The initial sale of a new issue of stock. Sales are usually from a broker who is one of the underwriters of the issue, and there should be no brokerage fee. Also called primary offering, *primary distribution*, and initial public offering.

initial offering *See* "new issue."

insider trading Trading in securities by an individual who could be privy to non-public information about those securities or the corporation whose securities they are. Such as person might be a member of the board of directors or a legal counsel for that corporation. Insider trading is considered unfair to the investing public and is against the law.

investment banker A broker who underwrites new issues of stock. Often a consortium of investment bankers buy all the new issue of a stock and then resell the shares at a markup.

investment company A corporation that invests in other companies. A closed-end investment company has a finite number of shares and they are sold through a stock exchange like the shares of any other corporation. An open-ended investment company can sell any number of shares, but it must stand ready to buy any number of those shares back from investors on demand. An open-ended investment company is called a *mutual fund*.

leveraged buyout The acquisition of a company primarily with borrowed money.

liabilities All debts and other claims against a corporation including its obligation to pay interest, dividends, taxes, and salaries.

limited liability *See* "corporation."

liquidity The ease with which a market can satisfy all demands for buying or selling securities or commodities. Insufficient liquidity can force prices unnecessarily high or low.

long Indicates ownership. Used in contrast to *short* which means not to own.

margin The amount of cash or securities required to be left on deposit with a broker as collateral for the purchase of other securities on credit. Margin requirements are regulated by the SEC.

margin account A type of account that an investor may hold with a brokerage in which cash or securities on deposit allow the investor to purchase other securities on credit. A margin account is necessary for all short sales.

market maker A brokerage firm that buys and sells specific over-the-counter issues for its own account. The brokerage posts its bid and asked prices for those securities on the NASDAQ quotation system. The market maker is the over-the-counter equivalent of the exchange specialist. If you buy stocks and your broker is a market maker for that stock, then you may either pay a markup (when the broker acts as principal) or a commission (when the broker acts as agent). Your broker will usually offer whichever of the two alternatives is cheaper.

merger The friendly takeover of one corporation by another.

minus tick A security transaction that takes place at a price below that of the previous transaction.

money-market funds A mutual fund that only invests in short-term debt securities called *money-market instruments*. The shares are usually priced at one dollar.

money-market instruments Debt securities with maturities of not more than one year. These include treasury bills, certificates of deposit, banker's acceptances, and corporate commercial paper.

mutual fund An open-ended investment company that can sell any number of its own shares and must stand ready to redeem them on demand. All revenue from the sale of shares is invested in other companies. Shares are not sold on an exchange.

NASD *see* National Association of Securities Dealers.

NASDAQ The quotation service for over-the-counter securities. Stands for National Association of Securities Dealers Automated Quotations.

National Association of Securities Dealers (NASD) The regulatory body for over-the-counter securities, an association of brokers who deal with U.S. securities.

net change The difference between the current closing price and the closing price of the previous trading period. Usually the last column in newspaper stock quotations.

new issue A stock or other security being offered to the public for the first time. Also called an *initial offering*. Proceeds from initial offerings go to the issuing corporation.

NYSE New York Stock Exchange.

odd lot A number of shares less than one hundred, that is, less than a *round lot*.

odd lot differential A fraction of a point sometimes added to the price of odd-lot purchases.

open-end investment company A mutual fund.

OTC Over-the-counter.

oversubscribed A new issue when there are more buy orders than shares to sell. Usually all orders are reduced proportionally until the number of securities available is reached. Such securities almost always increase in value as soon as they begin to trade on the secondary market. In a takeover or an offer to repurchase stock (made by the issuing company) there are more offers to sell shares than the corporation has offered to buy.

over-the-counter (OTC) The market for all securities not listed on an exchange. Trades are made broker-to-broker on the telephone. Price quotations are from NASDAQ.

par value A value assigned to shares for bookkeeping purposes that has nothing to do with a stock's market value.

participating preferred stock An issue of preferred stock which might have its dividend increased if the dividend of the common shares has been met.

penny stock Shares that sell for under $3 a share or, according to some, under $5 a share. Issues in this category are extremely speculative.

P-E ratio *See* "price-earnings ratio."

pink sheets A list of over-the-counter stocks, their market makers, and their current bid and asked prices. These are stocks that are not carried in the regular NASDAQ listings.

plus tick *See* "up tick."

portfolio The total collection of securities held by an investor or institution.

preferred stock A stock issue with features that common stock doesn't have like a (usually) high dividend, or sometimes extra voting rights, or a prior claim on the assets of the issuing corporation in case of dissolution. Dividends are often cumulative and have precedence over the dividends of common shares. Preferred stock does not participate in earnings and does not represent equity ownership.

price-earnings ratio (p-e-ratio) The ratio of the per-share price of a stock to the per-share earnings of the company, or how many times the per-share price exceeds the per-share earnings. A corporation that does not have a net profit has no p-e ratio.

primary distribution *See* "initial distribution."

prime rate The interest rate that banks charge their most creditworthy customers.

principal In a securities transaction the broker is the agent for the customer who is the principal.

profit taking The selling of securities for capital gain. Usually applied to securities that have not been held for a long time or to an increase of selling after the crest of a rally.

proxy contest The attempt of persons, usually dissident shareholders, to obtain proxies from a large number of other shareholders so as to affect a corporate vote or even take over a corporation.

PSE The Pacific Stock Exchange.

quote or **quotation** Current market price or prices of a security as appears in newspapers, on quote terminals, or ticker displays. Prices quoted may be transaction prices, bid and ask prices, or highs and lows for the trading period covered. Other information is often given like volume, p-e ratio, and net change from the previous closing price.

record date *See* "holder of record."

red herring The prospectus of a new issue which must be in the hands of investors before they can purchase that security. Warnings concerning the risks of the security are printed in red on the first page.

registered representative A person who has passed the "Series 7" examination and is licensed to buy and sell securities. Registered reps are employed in brokerages to manage customer accounts. Sometimes they are called *account executives*.

retained earnings That part of a corporation's earnings not disbursed to the shareholders as dividends. Growth stocks usually retain all their earnings.

reverse stock split *See* "split."

right A right permits the investor to purchase additional shares of the underlying security at a set price for a limited amount of time. New issues often come in units consisting of one share with either rights or warrants attached.

round lot The standard unit of stock transactions, usually 100 shares. High-priced securities, occasionally trade in 10, 25, or 50-share round lots.

SEC *See* "Securities and Exchange Commission."

secondary distribution The subsequent sale of a large amount of stock still held by the issuing company or one of the large share-holders. Also, when a company issues more shares of stock after passing a corporate resolution.

secondary market The trading of securities after the primary distribution. Purchases are from prior owners of the stock, and the corporation gets no revenue from these sales. Stock exchanges are set up for the secondary market in stocks and other securities.

securities A general term which includes stocks, bonds, treasuries, and options.

Securities and Exchange Commission (SEC) A government agency set up to regulate the securities industry.

sell short The practice of selling a security before you own it so as to lock in that sale price. The investor is expected to purchase the security at a later date, and (hopefully) at a lower price so as to reimburse the broker who delivered the stock at the time of the short sale. The difference between the first sale and the subsequent purchase is the investor's profit after deducting expenses. A short sale is permitted only after an *up tick*.

share *See* "stock."

shareholder's equity Book value.

short In the position of not owning a security. Used in the context of selling short.

short against the box The same as short selling except that the investor owns the stock all along, as collateral. A less risky speculation than outright short selling.

specialist A member of the stock exchange to whom specific securities have been assigned. The specialist is charged with maintaining an orderly market in those securities. Often buying and selling for their own accounts, specialists must balance supply and demand so as to keep price movements in their securities minimal.

speculator The difference between an investor and a speculator is mostly of degree. The speculator is usually willing to take on higher risk and to trade more frequently than is the investor. This is done, of course, in the hopes of higher profit.

split A division of shares into a greater number, often done to reduce the per-share price. In the usual 2-for-1 split the investor would own twice as much stock as before and each share would be worth half as much. The number of shares may also be consolidated by a *reverse stock split*.

spread The difference between the bid and ask price. For thinly traded stock the spread will be greater than normal.

stock A unit of ownership in a corporation. Also called a share.

stock exchange An organized market place that provides the facilities for brokers to buy and sell securities. Usually, only securities registered on an exchange can be traded on that exchange. Trading is done at one location as opposed to the over-the-counter market which can be between two brokers at any two locations.

stockholder of record *See* "holder of record."

stockholder's equity *See* "book value."

street name The procedure whereby the stock certificates of an investor are held by his or her broker.

technical analysis A study of the price fluctuations of a security for the purpose of anticipating future price movement. Usually thought of in opposition to *fundamental analysis*.

technical rally A small rise in the price of a security following a much greater decline, usually the result of factors other than a fundamental change in the outlook for the security. Not expected to alter the continued downward trend.

tender offer A public offering to buy the shares of a target corporation at a stated price. Usually tender offers are for the purpose of taking control of a corporation.

thin market A condition whereby there is little demand for the purchase or sale of a security. A wider-than-normal gap appears between the bid and ask prices, and sudden demand can swing prices abruptly one way or the other.

third market Trading by brokers among themselves of a security listed on an exchange. Usually permitted only for large transactions.

tick The minimum amount by which a security price may move up or down. The higher priced the security the larger the tick will be.

ticker On-line transaction price reporting from the exchanges. Every transaction appears on the ticker now most commonly seen on cable TV or on ticker display boards at brokerages.

TSE Toronto Stock Exchange.

unit New issues are sometimes sold in units which contain one share with a right or warrant attached for the purchase of additional stock.

underwriter Investment banker.

up tick A security transaction price that takes place at a price greater than the previous price.

volume The amount of shares traded in a specified period.

warrant The right to buy stock of a specific issue at a stipulated price. Often attached to the shares of new issues.

yield Dividend from a stock, interest from a bond. In quotations, often expressed as a percentage of the current purchase price.